The Pocket Essential

Simpsons

www.pocketessentials.com

First published in Great Britain 2000 by Pocket Essentials, 18 Coleswood Rd, Harpenden, Herts, AL5 1EQ

Distributed in the U.S.A. by Trafalgar Square Publishing, P.O.Box 257, Howe Hill Rd, North Pomfret, Vermont 05053

A CIP catalogue record for this book is available from the British Library.

ISBN 1-903047-09-9

9 8 7 6 5 4 3 2

Book typeset by DP Fact & Fiction.
Printed and bound by Cox & Wyman

for Crow and the kids (again) pointing out my dreadful paucity of friends...

Contents

Introduction

Welcome to the best Simpsons book for those of you who wish to limit the damage to your pocket! I'm no fool – there are books out there that are bigger, more colourful, are official and have more detail. I'd be a mug to deny it – all I can do is nod my head gracefully, try not to become bitter and twisted at the thought of their production values and the size of their authors' advances, and specify the virtues of my own small volume. So what *are* these hypothetical virtues? They are (and feel free to sort them into the order of your choice):

■ This is the only book that covers series eleven. I realise that this is subject to change, but hopefully not anytime soon.

■ This book gives the UK reader an insight into what the BBC and SKY consider worth censoring in *The Simpsons*. This is not complete (especially as SKY have now started showing uncensored versions of shows they originally cut) but it gives you a good guide as to what will go missing now the BBC have decided the show is a kids show and have started to show episodes during *Live and Kicking* on a Saturday morning.

■ You get a handy pocket guide, which is more than anyone else can claim (see how quickly my 'unique differentiators' degrade).

■ It's quick to read. Not a big point with most people, but if you're on your deathbed and 'learn all the blackboard gags from *The Simpsons*' is on your list of things to do before you croak (see *One Fish, Two Fish, Blowfish, Blue Fish* for the genesis of this gag). I fancy I've made my point.

■ Most book are too thick to steady a table with a short leg. Not this one.

That was short and sweet, eh?

There's always a mission behind every book, and the mission behind this one is to provide you with a good guide to the series I love and a decent entry point to all the attractive merchandise you can waste considerably more than the cost of this book on. I think I've achieved this – if you agree/disagree/want to point out errors you can get me at pmann@pdillonp.freeuk.com, or via the publisher's address that is listed somewhere in this volume.

Now, the people who made this possible...

Matt Groening – the man responsible

Matt Groening changed the look of television when he created the first animated primetime series in twenty years with *The Simpsons*.

Groening (rhymes with 'raining') worked in a sewage treatment plant, as a chauffeur and a ghost-writer before he launched his cynical and very successful *Life in Hell* comic strip (at a bookshop near you, now). *Life in Hell* contains familiar (in both senses of the word) elements for Simpsons fans. The Simpsons debuted as shorts in 1987's Emmy Award-winning series *The Tracey Ullman Show*, and when *The Simpsons* was spun off into its own series it was the fledgling Fox Network's highest-rated programme. The Simpsons are named after Groening's own relatives: Groening's father and son are named Homer, his other son is named Abraham, his mother is Marge, and he has two sisters, Lisa and Maggie. Bart is an anagram of 'brat.'

In 1993 he formed Bongo Comic Group (named after one of the rabbits in *Life Is Hell*) which publishes various Simpsons Comics including *Itchy & Scratchy Comics*, *Bartman*, *Radioactive Man*, *Lisa Comics* and *Krusty Comics*. In 1995 he founded Zongo Comics to publish *Jimbo* and *Fleener*. He lives in Los Angeles where he produces his weekly strip, works on the series, runs Bongo and oversees the licensing and merchandising of *The Simpsons*. In 1999 a Simpsons comic strip was started, and has already been pulled from the Chicago Sun-Times due to it being, well, like *The Simpsons*. Also in 1999 Groening started a new series, *Futurama*, which is excellent and at the time of writing still getting better. A subject for another book, I hope...

Homer J Simpson

At various times husband, father, Safety Inspector at the Springfield Nuclear Power Plant, bowler, beer drinker, missionary, astronaut, Internet start-up entrepreneur amongst others. Abe 'Grandpa' Simpson raised Homer in the absence of his radical hippie mother. Married to his high school sweetheart, Marge Bouvier, Homer raises his three precious children in Evergreen Terrace.

Likes: Duff Beer, donuts, pork chops, Truckosaurus, hog fat, unprocessed fish sticks... well, you get the idea.

Dislikes: Monty Burns (who has an ability to forget Homer's very existence), work, Ned Flanders, work...

Emmy Award-winning (1992 and 1993) actor Dan Castellaneta (born 1958) voices Homer. He is also the voice of the Genie in the successful animated television series *Aladdin* and in the second sequel, *Return of Jaffar*. He has forged a body of work in animation, including Grandpa in *Hey Arnold!*, Flem in *Cow and Chicken*, Earthworm Jim in *Earthworm Jim* as well as appearing in video games from *Toonstruck* to *Planetscape: Torment*.

Castellaneta has had a long career in television as a regular on the ABC series *Sibs* and has been in shows such as *LA Law*, *NYPD Blue*, *Wings*, *Murphy Brown*, *Friends*, *Cybill*, *The Drew Carey Show*, *Love and War*, *The George Carlin Show* and *Married with Children*. His film work covers television films such as *Hand in the Glove* and the remake of Disney's *The Computer Wore Tennis Shoes* and the feature films *Nothing in Common, K9, War of the Roses, The Client, Space Jam, Forget Paris, Family Bloom* and *My Giant*.

Castellaneta is also an accomplished stage actor who spent four years with the famous Chicago Improvisational group The Second City and whose classical credits include *Taming of the Shrew, A Midsummer Night's Dream* and *Macbeth*. He starred as cantankerous comic book writer Harvey Pekar in *American Splendor* in Los Angeles in 1991 and in 1992 and 1993 performed with his wife, Deb Lacusta, in *Deb and Dan's Show* at different clubs in Santa Monica. He has also won a Drama League Award for his performance in *Tom and Jerry* as part of the Met Theater's 1994 One Act Festival.

As well as Homer, Dan plays: Krusty the Clown, Grandpa Simpson, Barney Gumble, Itchy (a mouse) Mayor Quimby, Groundskeeper Willy, Scott Christian, Freddy Quimby, Hans Moleman, Arnie Pie, Sideshow Mel, Kodos.

Marge Simpson

What can be said about Marge Simpson that hasn't been? Combining the role of homemaker and mother of three with not one, but many careers (all at different times). Police officer, protester, environmental activist, pretzel franchisee, real estate saleswoman… how can she find the time?

Likes: Homer, Bart, Lisa, Maggie, Patty, Selma, Grandpa(?).

Dislikes: Rather annoyingly tries to see the good in everyone.

The voice of Marge Simpson, Julie Kavner (born 1951) is probably best known in the UK for her supporting role as Brenda Morgenstern in the situation comedy *Rhoda*, for which she won an Emmy in 1987. She seems to have spent half her like being nominated for Emmy's – four for *Rhoda*, another four for *The Tracey Ullman Show* (1987-1990) and one for the daytime special *The Girl Who Couldn't Lose* in 1975, and has a raft of other TV credits.

She is a regular member of the cast of Woody Allen's movies including *New York Stories, Oedipus Wrecks, Radio Days, Hannah and Her Sisters, Alice, Shadows and Fog* and *Deconstructing Harry*. She appeared in the feature films *Surrender, National Lampoon Goes to the Movies*, and *Bad Medicine* as well as Nora Ephron's 1992 feature film *This Is Your Life* and co-starred with Robert DeNiro and Robin Williams in the 1990 film *Awakenings*.

As well as Marge, Julie's characters include Patty, Selma, and Grandma Bouvier.

Bart Simpson

Thought of as an underachiever and troublemaker, Bart is better than he (or most of the people who come into contact with him) would like to think. He can always be relied on to do the right thing, usually at the last moment and under duress. He's had a TV series (no, not *The Simpsons*, the one with Krusty the Clown in *Bart Gets Famous*) had a comet named after him (*Bart's Comet*) caught Springfield's most notorious criminal five times (five out of six Sideshow Bob episodes – the last time was a technicality) and been heralded as an inspiration for the entire town (*Bart's Inner Child*). Let's not mention the top ten hit *Do The Bartman*. If this is underachieving we should all be so afflicted.

Likes: Radioactive Man, Santa's Little Helper, Marge, Lisa and Homer, Milhouse, the entire L'il Bastard line of toys, everything Krusty.

Dislikes: Lisa, Homer (hey, 'a foolish consistency is the hobgoblin of little minds'), Sideshow Bob, authority.

Bart's voice is by Emmy Award-winning actress and voice-over artist Nancy Cartwright (born 1959), who toured the US on the stage from the age of 12. She studied with Daws Butler, the voice of Yogi Bear, Huckleberry Hound and other Hanna-Barbera greats. Her television appearances include characters in the animated shows *Richie Rich, Mike Lu and Og, Animaniacs, Big Guy and Rusty the Boy Robot*, and *God, the Devil and Bob* as well as live action appearances on *Not My Kid, Rules of Marriage, Deadly Lessons, Fame, Miss Rose White, Empty Nest, Cheers, The Fresh Prince of Bel Air* and *Baywatch Nights*. At the movies Nancy has appeared in *Twilight Zone: The Movie, Flesh and Blood, Undercover, The Great O'Grady,* and *Godzilla*. She has also developed and toured her one-woman show, *In Search of Fellini,* which premiered in Los Angeles.

As well as Bart, Nancy's characters include Nelson Muntz, Rod & Todd Flanders, Kearney and Mrs. Wiggum.

Lisa Simpson

Definitely a 'brainiac' Lisa's the soul of the family. An adept sax player under the personal tuition of the now deceased 'Bleeding Gums' Murphy she enjoys writing essays, attending school and reading magazines about boys (of the non-threatening kind) Lisa is a vegetarian and, if prophecy is to be believed, will be President one day.

Likes: Several actors all called Corey, Malibu Stacy, Lisa Lionheart, sensitive teachers, vegetarianism.

Dislikes: How long have you got? Injustice, basically…

The voice of Lisa, Yeardley Smith, was born in Paris in 1964 and later moved to Washington, D.C., where she grew up. She began her career at 14 playing Tinkerbell in a musical adaptation of *Peter Pan*. While enjoying a successful stage career she appeared in her first two movies: *Heaven Help Us* and *The Legend of Billie Jean*. In 1986 she moved to Los Angeles, where she won the part of Lisa Simpson on

The Tracey Ullman Show.

She's also appeared in *Dharma & Greg, Murphy Brown, Empty Nest, Tales from the Dark Side, Mama's Family,* and played Louise Fitzer for three years on Fox's *Herman's Head*. Other films include *City Slickers, Maximum Overdrive* and *As Good As It Gets.*

Maggie Simpson

For a one year old Maggie isn't doing badly – she's instigated a crusade against violence on TV, shot Springfield's richest man because he attempted to steal her lollipop, communed with bears, wandered the town alone and led a baby rebellion. Intends to learn how to walk and talk right about... now. Or not.

Likes: Pacifiers.

Dislikes: Who knows what scary thoughts go on in that head?

Abe 'Grandpa' Simpson

Abe Simpson is a veteran of the Second World War, who participated in a tontine for stolen artworks with Montgomery Burns. Father to Homer, grandfather to Bart, Lisa, and Maggie, Abe lives in the Springfield Retirement Castle. As well as fronting for Bart and Lisa as a writer for the award-winning Itchy & Scratchy cartoon series (*The Front*), Abe is also the inventor of a sex tonic that actually works (*Grandpa versus Sexual Inadequacy*). Mostly though he just stands around looking baffled.

Likes: Soft food, quoits, telling stories, medication.

Dislikes: Homer's Mom (he still wants to sleep with her though).

Patty and Selma Bouvier

Although on the face of it Patty and Selma are identical twins they are in fact very, very different, but only in Patty being less desperate than her sister, Selma, who has been married and divorced twice.

Selma married Sideshow Bob straight out of prison for framing Krusty the Clown and he promptly tried to blow her up on their honeymoon. Her second marriage was to Troy McClure to restore his reputation after a scandal involving fish, but ended when Selma and Troy realised they didn't love each other. Selma's hottest relationship now is her custodial one with Jub Jub, her pet iguana. Having said that Patty did have a relationship with Principal Skinner (*Principal Charming*).

Likes: Cigarettes. Lots of cigarettes. MacGyver.

Dislikes: Homer Simpson, being single, Homer Simpson.

Pets

Snowball I

Homer and Marge tried to fool Lisa by replacing this deceased feline with the identical Snowball II. Mentioned in a letter in *Simpsons Roasting on an Open Fire.*

Snowball II

The replacement for the Simpson family's first cat. A gifted beastie, she gets on well with Santa's Little Helper.

Santa's Little Helper

Santa's Little Helper was unlucky at the racetrack but lucky that Christmas when he joined the Simpsons (*Simpsons Roasting on An Open Fire*). In his owner, Bart Simpson, Santa's Little Helper has the most tolerant dog-owner of the modern age. He's had children (25 to be precise – see *Two Dozen and One Greyhounds*) and has earned a degree from one of Springfield's most prestigious canine academies (*Bart's Dog Gets An F*). True, bad things have happened – he was briefly abandoned in favour of Laddie (*The Canine Mutiny*) and he and Snowball II were ignored in favour of an Elephant (*Bart Gets An Elephant*) but he's weathered good and bad with a tolerance bordering on the imbecilic.

Other Cast Members

We've covered most of the cast members with their characters above. Here are two more stalwarts who make the show what it is:

Harry Shearer

Harry Shearer (born 1943) has been acting for so long that he's a natural for the voice of Monty Burns. He started at seven and hasn't stopped, taking in classic movie comedy (*Abbott and Costello Go to Mars*), the first CinemaScope movie (*The Robe*), the early days of TV (*The Jack Benny Show, GE Theatre* and *Alfred Hitchcock Presents*), even playing the role of Eddie Haskell in the pilot episode of *Leave It to Beaver.*

As one of the creators and stars of *This Is Spinal Tap,* Shearer gained national recognition as Derek Smalls and joined the cast and writers of *Saturday Night Live* for two seasons.

Recent films include *The Right Stuff, The Fisher King, The Truman Show, Small Soldiers* and *Godzilla,* and he has won awards for his work on television, where he has worked as actor, director and writer on shows, including Martin Mull's *Portrait of a White Marriage, HBO Comedy Hour Live: The Magic of Live, Fernwood 2 Night, Ellen, Murphy Brown, LA Law, Chicago Hope, ER, The Visitor,* and *The News Hole.*

With Tom Leopold and Peter Matz he wrote a comedy musical about J Edgar Hoover and has recorded a two-CD compilation, *O.J. on Trial: The Early Years* and *O.J. on Trial: That Endless Summer*, containing selected excerpts from his nationally syndicated radio show, entitled *Le*

Show. Le Show has become on of the top public radio shows since it began 15 years ago, and is available on the Internet weekly at *www.harryshearer.com*.

Harry's characters include Montgomery Burns, Smithers, Principal Skinner, Dr. Marvin Monroe (deceased), Otto (the school bus driver), Reverend Lovejoy, Ned Flanders, Dr. Julius Hibbert, Kent Brockman, Dr. Pryor, Eddie, Herman, Mr. Largo, Jasper, McBain, George Bush, Lenny, Dave Sutton, Richard Nixon, Scratchy (a cat), Jebediah Springfield, Kang and others.

Hank Azaria

Hank (born 1964) studied at the American Academy of Dramatic Arts in New York, playing Hamlet in a production of *Rosencrantz and Guildenstern Are Dead* at Columbia University. He's continued with stage work playing in *Uncle Vanya, The Merchant of Venice, The Ballad of the Sad Café* and *The Dumb Waiter*.

In Los Angeles he experimented with improv and sketch comedy and was a favourite at the local comedy clubs. Azaria won a Drama League Award for his performance in the play *Conspicuous Consumption*. Recent films include *Cradle Will Rock, Grosse Pointe Blank, Godzilla, Homegrown, The Birdcage, Now and Then, Great Expectations, Heat, Quiz Show* and the voice of Bartok in *Anastasia*.

Sadly, given all this talent, Azaria is best known for his recurring role as Nat the dog walker on *Mad About You*...

Hank's characters include Moe, Apu, Police Chief Wiggum, Lou, Carl Smith, Dr. Nick Riviera, Professor Frink, Akira, Snake, Cletus, Kirk Van Houten, Superintendent Chalmers and many others.

Other regular 'guest voices' are provided by...

Marcia Wallace is the voice of Edna Krabappel; Russi Taylor is Martin Prince (and others); Milhouse is voiced by Pamela Hayden who also does Rod Flanders, Janey Powell and Dolph amongst others; Tess MacNeille provides the voice of Jimbo and Dolph on occasions, as well as Agnes Skinner and others; Maggie Roswell is Maude Flanders (soon RIP) and Helen Lovejoy and others; and Doris Grau (1924 – 1995), was Lunchlady Doris as well as a script supervisor on the show.

Probably the 'guest voice' that will be most missed from the show is that of Phil Hartman (1948-1998) the voice of, amongst other people, Troy McClure. Hartman's tragic death shouldn't be dwelt on in a book like this but Hartman was a great asset to the show, moving from McClure to Moses, Charlton Heston, Lionel Hutz and a variety of scoundrels of a greater or lesser degree. Phil appeared (usually as a slightly unsavoury, self-interested character) in scores of films and TV shows such as *Small Soldiers* and the hit comedy TV show *News Radio.* He will be greatly missed.

The Simpsons shorts on The Tracey Ullman Show

I'd guess that few of us in the UK have seen these shorts. They are crude by the standards we now expect from *The Simpsons,* and don't have the same voices, or even names we now expect. Castellaneta says *"(The voice) doesn't take a lot of effort now, but in the beginning it was hard to try to find a voice. The one I settled on was just easier to do for a half-hour."* In fact Homer's early voice in even the first season of the half hours shows sounds much more 'real' in a gruff-dad-sitcom sort of way. Marge (although described as Marge) is never referred to as Marge, and for most of the episodes Homer is called 'Dad', as in 'Bart and Dad Eat Dinner'. The Simpsons Complete Guide renames these shorts – 'Bart and Dad Eat Dinner' is called 'Bart and Homer Eat Dinner', but that's not how they went out. The characterisation is different. Lisa isn't as intelligent as she becomes during the series, but is more like a younger Bart. Maggie speaks (albeit in a high pitched voice that is often gibberish). Homer and Marge are both more conventional than they are in the series and Homer is more intelligent, although also more belligerent. Bart, however, seems to have sprung fully formed, with the exception of how many spikes he has on his head – it began as 13 and ended up as 7. Go on, count them. All transmission dates refer to the US showing.

First Season (1987)

Good Night, April 19 1987

Attempting to settle the kids off to sleep, Dad and Mom invite philosophy and trauma as Bart ponders the nature of consciousness, Lisa is terrified that the bedbugs really *do* bite and Maggie takes "Rock-A-Bye Baby" *way* too literally.

Watching Television, May 3 1987

Bart and Lisa argue about what channel to watch, but can only agree on shouting at Maggie when she tries to change stations.

Bart Jumps, May 10 1987

Dad imparts a trust lesson to Bart, when he tries to get him to jump into his arms. Every time Bart tries, Homer's gone.

Babysitting Maggie, May 31 1987

Bart and Lisa watch TV as Maggie electrocutes herself, falls down the stairs and chases a butterfly along – and off – the roof.

The Pacifier – June 21 1987

Trying to remove Maggie's pacifier is a thankless task for Bart and Lisa.

Burp Contest – June 28 1987

Despite Marge's objections a burping contest is held.

Eating Dinner – July 12 1987

"Good drink... good meat... good God, let's eat!" This is Homer's version of Grace before the family attack the purple goop that Marge has lovingly served them.

Second Season (1987-88)

Making Faces, September 22 1987

Despite Mom's warning that they'll freeze that way forever, the kids make scary faces.

The Funeral, October 4 1987

Bart anticipates seeing his first dead body at Uncle Hubert's funeral, but passes out when he does.

Maggie's Brain, October 11 1987

While Bart and Lisa wonders what Maggie is thinking we see them from her point of view: first as demons, then as infants like herself who she can tickle.

Football, October 18 1987

If Bart can catch one of Homer's passes it's Frosty Chocolate Milkshakes all round... uh-oh, look out for that cliff...

House of Cards, October 25 1987

Bart is building a giant house of cards despite Lisa and Maggie's distractions.

Bart and Dad Eat Dinner, November 1 1987

Marge and Lisa are at the ballet, so Bart and Homer must feed themselves. Be afraid...

Space Patrol, November 8 1987

Bartron, a berserk Martian robot (looking uncannily like Bart with a vase stuck on his head) is attacking Earth. Our only hope is space pilot Lisuey and her sidekick Mageena!

Bart's Haircut, November 15 1987

Bart can have any haircut he likes – as long as it's bald.

World War III, November 22 1987

Homer prepares everyone for the apocalypse – by waking everybody up for a nuclear attack drill... again and again.

The Perfect Crime, December 13 1987

Cookie-stealing Bart thinks Maggie will be blamed for his crimes. Stuffed, he lies amongst the tell-tale crumbs.

Scary Stories, December 20 1987

Bart tells Lisa and Maggie scary stories in the dark, and they appear to be coming true...

Grandpa and the Kids, January 10 1988

Having bored Lisa and Bart rigid with his stories Grandpa then feigns his own death.

Introducing: Grandpa Simpson

Gone Fishin', January 24 1988

After a hearty worm sandwich Bart and Homer have a swift ride down the rapids in an unconventional fishing trip.

Skateboarding, February 7 1988

It's skateboard hell as Bart, Lisa, and Maggie take to the streets.

The Pagans, February 14 1988

Bart, Lisa, and Maggie annoy Homer and Marge by converting to paganism on the way to church.

The Closet, February 21 1988

Avoiding chores Bart hides in the closet, and gets locked in, missing a trip to get Frosty Chocolate Milkshakes.

The Aquarium, February 28 1988

Bart takes a dip in the shark tank on a trip to the Aquarium.

Family Portrait, March 6 1988

Homer's attempts to get a family photograph seem doomed to failure.

Bart's Hiccups, March 13 1988

Bart's hiccups are subject to treatment by Doctor Lisa and Nurse Maggie – a cure worse than the affliction.

The Money Jar, March 20 1988

Internal struggle ahead for Lisa, Bart and Maggie as they are tempted by Marge's money in the cookie jar.

The Art Museum, May 1 1988

Homer and Marge's suspicions that the kids aren't ready for culture are confirmed at the Art Gallery by Bart's early specialisation in the nude.

Zoo Story, May 8 1988

At the Zoo the Simpsons find an eerily familiar monkey family.

Third Season (1988-89)

In this season the shorts are shown as a single story rather than being divided into sections.

Shut Up Simpsons, November 6 1988

It's argumentarama with Grandpa, Homer, and the kids.

The Shell Game, November 13 1988

Trying to hide a stolen cookie from his parents, Bart ends up playing the Shell Game.

The Bart Simpson Show, November 20 1988

When Homer tells Bart and Lisa to stop watching *Itchy & Scratchy*, Bart pulls out the picture tube, gets into the TV set and puts on his own show.

Introducing: Itchy & Scratchy

Punching Bag, November 27 1988

Lisa helps Bart with his punching by drawing Dad's face on the punching bag. Strangely he's not the only family member to be inspired to greater levels of violence by it.

Simpson Xmas, December 18 1988

To the strains of *The Night Before Christmas*, Bart narrates a tale of Christmas present peeking.

The Krusty the Clown Show, January 15 1989

The kids go to see the live recording of Krusty the Clown's show; Bart is disappointed to find that Krusty is *"Just some guy in clown makeup."*

Bart the Hero, January 29 1989

Sent out for exercise, Bart visits the candy store and accidentally foils a robbery.

Bart's Little Fantasy, February 5 1989

Instructed to clean up his room Bart has a role reversal fantasy about himself, his siblings and his parents.

Scary Movie, February 12 1989

Bart persuades his sisters to see *Revenge of the Space Mutants* instead of *Return of the Happy Little Elves.*

Home Hypnotism, February 19 1989

Trying to calm the kids by using hypnosis, Homer and Marge apparently turn them into zombies instead.

Shoplifting, February 26 1989

Bart's master plan to steal some chocolate fails.

Echo Canyon, March 12 1989

While taking a rest stop at Echo Canyon the family enjoy themselves and Bart nearly crushes the car with a boulder.

Bathtime, March 19 1989

Bart's bath time becomes the adventures of Bart Simpseau – but he leaves the water running.

Bart's Nightmare, March 26 1989

A dreaming Bart is pursued by cookies out to eat him.

Bart of the Jungle, April 16 1989

Bart, Lisa, and Maggie recreate Tarzan's vine-swinging lifestyle – with Homer's ties.

Family Therapy, April 23 1989

Homer uses Frosty Chocolate Milkshakes to get the family to a psychologist to find out why they don't laugh any more.

Maggie in Peril: Chapter One, April 30 1989

Due to Bart and Lisa's inept babysitting Maggie chases her ball on Bart's skateboard all the way to a sewage pipe that leads to a waterfall. As she falls over the edge..."To be continued NEXT WEEK"

Maggie in Peril: the Thrilling Conclusion, May 7 1989

Maggie survives the fall and manages to get back home with the help of some helium balloons.

T.V. Simpsons, May 14 1989

Bart's kite hits the TV aerial and Homer has to climb to the roof in an attempt to restore his TV picture.

Season One (1990)

Some Enchanted Evening (7G01) 13 May 1990

Homer discovers that Marge is disillusioned with their marriage when she calls a radio shrink and tells him that their marriage is failing. Homer takes Marge out for a romantic evening at the Offramp Inn, leaving the kids with a babysitter – who is really a burglar featured that night on *America's Most Armed and Dangerous*.

Guest stars: Penny Marshall.

Blackboard: I will not yell "Fire" in a crowded classroom.

Couch: Everybody fits on the couch.

Phone Call For: Al...Al Coholic...is there an Al Coholic here? *And* Oliver Clothesoff! Call for Oliver Clothesoff!

Bart the Genius (7G02) 14 January 1990

Bart swaps his IQ test with Martin's, and ends up (to the astonishment of all) at a school for gifted children. It's not long before the downside of the situation makes itself evident.

Blackboard: I will not waste chalk.

Couch: Bart is squeezed off the couch and pops into the air; he is seen coming down in front of the TV as the opening credits end.

Homer's Odyssey (7G03) 21 January 1990

When Homer is fired for causing another accident at the nuclear plant, he almost commits suicide. At the crucial moment he undergoes a conversion to safety activist, and soon is picketing the plant he was fired from.

Introducing: Montgomery Burns and Smithers.

Blackboard: I will not skateboard in the halls.

Couch: The couch falls apart because everybody is crushed together on it.

Phone Call For: Uh, is I.P. Freely here? Hey, everybody, I.P. Freely!

There's No Disgrace Like Home (7G04) 28 January 1990

After a works picnic Homer realises that his family are not like other people. He sells the TV and makes for the family therapy centre of Dr Marvin Monroe, where shocking events will occur.

Introducing: Marvin Monroe.

Blackboard: I will not burp in class.

Couch: Homer is squeezed off his side of the couch.

Bart the General (7G05) 4 February 1990

Under the influence of cupcake, Bart defends Lisa from Nelson Muntz's bullying and ends up as the target of the bully. He asks Grandpa Simpson to help him and together with Herman at the militaria shop they organise a military campaign against Nelson.

Introducing: Otto, Herman (he of the military collectibles) and Nelson Muntz.

Moaning Lisa (7G06) 11 February 1990

A depressed Lisa meets just what she needs – a fellow blues musician, 'Bleedin' Gums' Murphy. Meanwhile Homer is involved in a desperate struggle to beat Bart at *Super Slugfest*.

Guest Stars: Ron Taylor.

Blackboard: I will not instigate revolution.

Couch: Maggie shoots into the air from the crush that is the family. Marge catches her and places her on her lap.

Phone Call For: Uh, Jacques Strap! Hey guys, I'm looking for a Jacques Strap!

What's been cut? If you see the scene with Homer and Bart playing *Super Slugfest* on SKY you'll get nine scenes of blood-drenched mayhem that have been cut from the BBC version.

The Telltale Head (7G07) 25 February 1990

To impress Jimbo and company Bart decapitates a statue of the town's founder, Jebediah Obediah Zacariah Jenadiah Springfield. Even Jimbo and henchmen are shocked and the entire town ends up in pursuit of Bart.

Introducing: Reverend Lovejoy and Sideshow Bob (in shot) not to mention slacker Jimbo.

Blackboard: I did not see Elvis.

Couch: Bart is squeezed off and pops into the air; he is seen coming down as the opening credits end.

The Simpsons Christmas Special (Simpsons Roasting on a Open Fire) (7G08) 17 December 1989

It's a miserable Christmas for the Simpsons: Monty Burns has cut the Christmas bonuses, Marge has spent the Christmas savings to erase

Bart's tattoo. To cover up the fact that he didn't get a bonus, Homer takes a second job as a store Santa.

Introducing: Patty and Selma, Santa's Little Helper and Ned and Todd Flanders.

The Call of the Simpsons (7G09) 18 February 1990

Acquiring a beat-up RV in response to Flanders' gleaming monster of a truck, Homer and the family head out for the wild. Lost (surprise!) and equipmentless, Bart and Homer go to get help, but end up in more of a state of nature than they want to be, and Homer is mistaken for Bigfoot.

Blackboard: I will not draw naked ladies in class.

Couch: Everybody fits on the couch.

Homer's Night Out (7G10) 25 March 1990

Bart acquires a mail order spy camera and catches Homer in mid-dance with a striptease artist at a stag party. When Bart's photo circulates through town Homer becomes a hero to the swingers in town, with a predictable reaction from Marge.

Blackboard: I will not call my teacher "Hot Cakes."

Couch: The couch falls apart underneath the family.

Life In The Fast Lane (7G11) 18 March 1990

When Homer gives Marge a bowling ball for her birthday, intending that she will let him use it a furious Marge vows to learn how to bowl. Her bowling teacher, the smoothly romantic Jacques tempts her to begin an affair...

Introducing: Helen Lovejoy.

Krusty Gets Busted (7G12) 29 April 1990

Homer witnesses Krusty the Clown robbing the Kwik-E-Mart, and Krusty is arrested. Bart vows to clear his hero's name, and places the blame where it belongs, with a master criminal who will return to haunt him.

Guest Stars: Kelsey Grammer.

Blackboard: They are laughing at me, not with me.

Couch: Maggie is squeezed off and pops into the air; she comes right down into Marge's arms.

The Crepes of Wrath (7G13) 15 April 1990

Tempted by the rosy prospect of being rid of Bart, Principal Skinner enrols Bart in a foreign exchange program. He ends up as the slave of some crooked wine makers who are using anti-freeze in their wine. The

Simpsons guest is Adil Hoaxha, an Albanian exchange student who is actually a spy.

Blackboard: Garlic gum is not funny.

Couch: Homer is squeezed off his side of the couch.

Season Two (1990-1991)

Two Cars in Every Garage, Three Eyes on Every Fish (7F01) 1 November 1990

Montgomery Burns decides to run for governor in order to keep his incredibly unsafe nuclear power plant from being closed down.

Blackboard: I will not Xerox my butt/It's potato, not potatoe (Used for the second airing of 7F01, this is a reference to Dan Quayle's educational ability.)

Introducing: Blinky, the three-eyed fish.

Couch: The couch unfolds into a bed.

Simpson and Delilah (7F02) 18 October 1990

Homer gets a hair regrowth formula charged to the company's health insurance. With his new luxurious mane Homer is promoted to an executive position, and helped and coached by his male secretary Karl, his irresistible rise begins...

Guest stars: Harvey Fierstein.

Blackboard: Tar is not a plaything.

Couch: The family do an Egyptian sand dance (well at least Wilson, Kepple and Betty's version of one) and sit on the couch with arms outstretched inviting applause.

Bart Gets An F (7F03) 11 October 1990

Bart is faced with having to repeat the fourth grade if he fails another test, and enlists the aid of Martin the class brain to help him pass.

Blackboard: I will not encourage others to fly/I will not fake my way through life.

Couch: The couch falls through the floor.

The Simpsons Halloween Special (Treehouse of Horror) (7F04) 25 October 1990

In their tree house Bart and Lisa swap tales of terror.

Bad Dream House

The Simpsons move into an Amityville-style haunted house, complete with a dimensional vortex, bleeding walls, and an Indian burial ground.

Hungry Are The Damned

The Simpsons are kidnapped by Aliens Kang and Kodos (in their first appearance) and are invited to a 'great feast' on Rigel 4.

The Raven

Edgar Allen Poe's classic tale is narrated with the Simpsons in starring parts, in a version that is very close to the original poem.

Guest Stars: James Earl Jones.

What's been cut? In the *Bad Dream House* segment SKY cut shots of the family members with knives, which the BBC showed uncut.

Dancin' Homer (7F05) 8 November 1990

After a drunken dance of encouragement at the baseball game, Homer becomes the mascot of the Springfield Isotopes. After his unique dancing exhibition helps them win a game Homer is offered a job with the Capital City Cardinals and they move to Capital City.

Guest stars: Tom Poston, Tony Bennett, who sings the Capital City song, a weird variant on *New York, New York*.

Blackboard: I will not trade pants with others.

Couch: Maggie ends up in Marge's hair.

Bart the Daredevil (7F06) 6 December 1990

Inspired by daredevil Captain Lance Murdock, Bart embarks on a life of death-defying feats culminating in him jumping Springfield Gorge on his skateboard. Homer rushes to save him, resulting in one of the funniest sequences (Homer down a hill, twice) to ever appear in *The Simpsons*.

First appearance: Doctor Hibbert.

Blackboard: I will not drive the principal's car.

Couch: Homer tips the couch over sideways; Maggie falls off, but lands on a couch cushion, which is on the floor.

What's been cut? This episode was produced in long and short versions, the short version having *Deep, Deep Trouble* from *Simpsons Sing The Blues* at the end. The BBC show the long version, SKY the short one, but rather perversely they show *Do The Bartman* at the end.

Bart vs. Thanksgiving (7F07) 22 November 1990

In an argument about where it should go, Bart consigns Lisa's thanksgiving centrepiece to the fire, and refuses to apologise about it. When he's sent to his room he runs away from home to a homeless shelter where he is filmed by a TV crew, alerting his family to where he is.

Blackboard: I will not do that thing with my tongue.

Couch: Grandpa is lying on the couch sleeping.

Dead Putting Society (7F08) 15 November 1990

Fuelled by parental rivalry Bart and Todd Flanders battle it out at the miniature golf tournament at Sir Putt-A-Lots. Homer and Ned Flanders have a side-bet – the father of the boy who loses mows the neighbour's lawn in their wife's Sunday dress.

Blackboard: I am not a 32 year old woman (a reference to Nancy Cartwright, the voice of Bart). *Couch:* Everybody fits onto the couch including Santa's Little Helper and Snowball II.

Itchy & Scratchy & Marge (7F09) 20 December 1990

When Maggie hits Homer in the head with a hammer after watching an Itchy and Scratchy cartoon Marge leads SNUH (Springfieldians for Non-violence, Understanding and Helping) and eliminates violence from cartoons. As a result Springfield enters a golden age, as children leave TV to play outside in the fresh air. When the same people want to ban Michelangelo's David, Marge must face up to the contradictions in her attitudes.

Blackboard: I will not pledge allegiance to Bart.

Couch: The couch is gone; everyone looks around at the empty spot.

Bart Gets Hit By A Car (7F10) 10 January 1991

When Mr. Burns hits Bart in an auto accident, and offers one hundred dollars compensation, Homer sues him. However they can only succeed if Bart is willing to lie about his injuries...

Introducing: The Devil and Lionel Hutz. No, really, the Devil *is* a recurring series character in *The Simpsons.*

Blackboard: I will not sell school property.

Couch: Homer bumps the others off the couch.

One Fish, Two Fish, Blowfish, Blue Fish (7F11) 24 January 1991

After eating improperly prepared blowfish at a sushi restaurant Homer believes that he has 24 hours to live. He makes a list of things he's got to do before dying, and spends the next day trying to achieve them.

Homer's List of Things to Do Before Dying: (Printed on "Dumb Things I Gotta Do Today" notepaper) 1. Make list (which is crossed out), 2. Eat a hearty breakfast, 3. Make videotape for Maggie, 4. Have man-to-man with Bart, 5. Listen to Lisa play her sax, 6. Make funeral arrangement, 7. Make peace with dad, 8. Beer with boys at the bar, 9. Tell off the boss, 10. Go hang gliding, 11. Plant a tree, 12. A final dinner with my beloved family, 13. Be intamit (*sic*) with Marge.

Guest Stars: George Takei and Larry King.

Blackboard: I will not cut corners (followed by ditto marks underneath).

Couch: The couch tips over backwards; Maggie pops up from behind it.

Phone Call For: Hey, is there a Butz here? Seymour Butz? Hey, everybody, I wanna Seymour Butz!

The Way We Was (7F12) 31 January 1991

When the Simpsons TV set breaks, Marge tells the kids how she and Homer first met in 1974 Springfield.

Introducing: McBain (or Rainier Wolfcastle if you prefer...)

Blackboard: I will not get very far with this attitude.

Couch: The couch falls through the floor.

Homer vs. Lisa and the 8th Commandment (7F13) 7 February 1991

When Homer gets an illegal cable hook-up he becomes a popular figure, especially on the night of the big fight. A thorn in the side is Lisa, who refuses to watch, for fear of losing her soul as it breaks the 8th Commandment.

Blackboard: I will not make flatulent noises in class.

Couch: The family do an Egyptian sand dance.

Bart's Dog Gets An F (7F14) 7 March 1991

After offences against Homer (including chewing up Homer's new $125 sneakers and the Bouvier family quilt) Bart must help Santa's Little Helper pass his final exam at obedience school, or lose him.

Guest Stars: Tracey Ullman.

Blackboard: I will not sell school property (same as *Bart Gets Hit By a Car*).

Couch: Everybody fits onto the couch including Santa's Little Helper and Snowball II.

What's been cut? Like *Bart the Daredevil* this episode was produced in long and short versions, the short version having *Deep, Deep Trouble* at the end. The BBC show the long version, SKY the short one.

Principal Charming (7F15) 14 February 1991

When Homer sets up a date between Principal Skinner and Marge's sister, Selma, he couldn't guess that Skinner would fall for Patty. As their relationship deepens, Bart takes full advantage.

Blackboard: I will not belch the National Anthem.

Couch: The couch unfolds into a bed.

Phone Call For: Uh, Homer Sexual? Aw, come on, come on, one of you guys has gotta be Homer Sexual!

Oh Brother, Where Art Thou? (7F16) 21 February 1991

After suffering a heart attack Grandpa Simpson tells Homer that he has a half-brother, Herbert Powell, a carmaker in Detroit. The two brothers are united and Herbert wants Homer, as the average American, to design a car for his car company, a decision he'll come to regret.

Guest Stars: Danny DeVito.

Blackboard: I will not sell land in Florida.

Couch: Maggie ends up in Marge's hair.

What's been cut? Bart referring to Herbert as a bastard in a sequence that mocks the idea of offensive language being dependent on context. The BBC cut it, SKY left it in.

Old Money (7F17) 28 March 1991

Grandpa Simpson inherits one hundred thousand dollars from his late girlfriend; he decides to give it to people who need it most. After interviewing hundreds of needy cases he realises that he needs more than $100,000 and heads for a casino to gamble for more money, with Homer in hot pursuit.

Guest Stars: Audrey Meadows.

Blackboard: I will not grease the monkey bars.

Couch: Grandpa is lying on the couch sleeping.

Brush with Greatness (7F18) 11 April 1991

Homer tackles his weight problem after becoming stuck in the water slide at the Mount Splashmore theme park, while Marge takes up painting and enrols in a class at Springfield Community College. Her painting of Homer asleep on the couch wins a competition and she finds herself commissioned to bring out the inner beauty of Monty Burns in a portrait for the Burns wing of the museum.

Guest Stars: Jon Lovitz, Ringo Starr as himself.

Blackboard: I will not hide behind the Fifth Amendment.

Couch: Homer tips the couch over sideways; Maggie falls off, but lands on a couch cushion, which is on the floor.

Lisa's Substitute (7F19) 25 April 1991

When Lisa's regular teacher falls sick she is replaced with a substitute teacher who imbues Lisa with a new love for learning, and even manages to persuade Homer of some of his duties as a father. Meanwhile the race is on: Bart against Martin for president of the class.

Couch: The couch is gone; everyone looks around the empty spot.

Guest Stars: Dustin Hoffman plays Mr. Bergstrom (uncredited). In the Complete Guide he's credited as 'Sam Etic' (semetic) which is a Jewish joke, I guess.

War Of The Simpsons (7F20) 2 May 1991

A drunken Homer ruins a party thrown by Marge and she signs herself and Homer up for Reverend Lovejoy's marriage counselling retreat at Catfish Lake. Catfish Lake means only one thing to Homer: fishing. Bart and Lisa are left in the company of Grandpa Simpson, who, despite having to suffer their party, has a trick up his sleeve.

Blackboard: I will not do anything bad ever again.

Couch: Homer bumps the others off the couch.

Three Men and a Comic Book (7F21) 9 May 1991

Bart, Martin and Milhouse pool resources in order to purchase the first *Radioactive Man* comic book for $100. None of its new owners are willing to let the rare book out of their sight, so they spend the night in Bart's treehouse, where Bart slowly gets crazier, in a *Treasure of the Sierra Madre* style.

Guest Stars: Cloris Leachman.

Blackboard: I will not show off (written in copperplate).

Couch: The couch tips backwards; Maggie pops up from behind it.

Blood Feud (7F22) 11 July 1991

When Bart is the only citizen of Springfield that can donate the double-O negative blood Mr. Burns needs, Homer expects more gratitude for Bart's donation than a thank-you note. He writes a vindictive note to Burns, and when he wakes the next day finds that Bart has posted the note. And Burns is not happy…

Blackboard: I will not sleep through my education.

Couch: The couch falls through the floor.

Phone Call For: Mike Rotch! Mike Rotch! Hey, has anybody seen Mike Rotch lately?

Season Three (1991-1992)

When Flanders Failed (7F23) 3 October 1991

Ned Flanders announces at a barbecue that he has quit his regular job and is opening a mall store catering to left handed people. Homer hopes that Flanders will fail, and on a visit to the Leftorium is pleased to see it empty. Flanders is near bankruptcy when Homer's better side shows through…

Blackboard: Nobody likes sunburn slappers.

Couch: The family do an Egyptian sand dance.

Stark Raving Dad (7F24) 19 September 1991

When Bart leaves his lucky red hat in a washer load of white shirts, Homer wears a pink shirt to work. Spotted as a dangerous pink-clad troublemaker by Monty Burns, with Bart's help he is soon committed to a mental institution. Here he meets a large white man who walks and talks like, and thinks he is, Michael Jackson.

Before transmission in the US this episode had a new sequence added, responding to President George Bush's comment that 'We need a nation closer to the Waltons than the Simpsons.' Bart's riposte? 'Hey, we're just like the Waltons. We're praying for an end to the depression, too!'

Guest Stars: Michael Jackson voices 'Michael' credited as John Jay Smith. Will the madness never end…

Blackboard: I am not a dentist.

Couch: The couch tips over backwards, and everybody crashes through the back wall.

Mr Lisa Goes To Washington (8F01) 26 September 1991

Lisa wins a Reading Digest Patriots of Tomorrow contest, and the Simpsons win a trip to Washington DC. When she sees her Congressman taking a bribe for a permit to cut down Springfield National Forest, her faith in democracy is shaken and she writes an essay exposing the congressman and condemning politicians in Washington.

Blackboard: Spitwads are not free speech.

Couch: Homer sits on Santa's Little Helper then pulls him out from beneath him.

Treehouse of Horror II (8F02) 31 October 1991

In what is to become a tradition Lisa, Bart, and Homer eat too much candy, and end up having nightmares… so, three more tales of horror…

The Monkey's Paw

On a foreign trip The Simpsons pick up a monkey's paw that gives the holder four wishes… a parody of WW Jacobs' classic horror story of the same name.

Bart The Monster

In a parody of the *Twilight Zone* episode 'It's a Good Life', everyone in Springfield lives in fear of Bart Simpson who is gifted with strange mental powers.

Homer's Brain

Homer's brain is transplanted into a robot worker by Monty Burns, who the Homer robot promptly falls on. In order for Burns to live his head needs a new host…

Phone Call For: Uh, hey, everybody! I'm a stupid moron with an ugly face and big butt and my butt smells and I like to kiss my own butt. Wait a minute…

What's been cut? On Sky the last scene of the episode, tagged on after the viewer believes the end credits have begun:

(Executive Producer credit appears.)

ANNOUNCER – "Next week on 'The Simpsons'…"

(scene at the breakfast table, including Homer with the head of Mr. Burns attached to his shoulder.)

LISA – "Don't forget Dad, tonight my class is having an all-you-can-eat spaghetti dinner."

HOMER – "Mmm… Spaghetti…"

BURNS' HEAD – "But Homer, tonight's our reception for Queen Beatrix of The Netherlands!"

HOMER – "Oh, I hate having two heads."

(end credits resume.)

Bart The Murderer (8F03) 10 October 1991

After a rotten day of school Bart and his skateboard barge into 'The Legitimate Businessman Social Club', where Fat Tony gives him a job as a bartender. When the mobsters find out that he is late at work because of Principal Skinner, Skinner disappears, and Bart is accused of his murder.

Guest Stars: Joe Mantegna and Neil Patrick Harris.

Blackboard: High explosives and school don't mix/I will not bribe Principal Skinner.

Couch: The family forms a pyramid.

Homer Defined (8F04) 17 October 1991

Homer becomes a hero when his panicky actions accidentally save the Springfield Nuclear plant. He is recruited to deliver a pep talk to the employees of an identical plant in Shelbyville, where he saves the plant by the same eeny-meeny-miny-moe method, this time observed by the other employees. His heroism is forgotten as 'pulling a Homer' is now a synonym for good results obtained via dumb luck.

Guest Stars: Magic Johnson and Chick Hearn.

Blackboard: I will not squeak chalk (written to squeaky chalk soundtrack).

Couch: An alien disappears through a trap door in the floor just before the family appears.

Like Father, Like Clown (8F05) 24 October 1991

While having dinner with the Simpsons to thank Bart for believing him (see *Krusty Gets Busted*) Krusty tells them his real name is Krustofsky, and he is estranged from his rabbi father, who disowned him when Krusty decided to be a clown instead of a rabbi. Bart attempts to reunite clown and rabbi.

Guest Stars: Jackie Mason as Rabbi Krustofsky.

Blackboard: I will finish what I sta (the rest of the blackboard is blank).

Couch: Bart lands across everyone's lap.

Lisa's Pony (8F06) 7 November 1991

After failing to supply Lisa with a reed for her Sax just before a recital due to an unscheduled stop-off at Moe's, Homer finally gives Lisa a pony as recompense. To pay off the money he's loaned for the pony, Homer works the graveyard shift at Apu's Kwik-E-Mart, slowly turning into a zombie.

Blackboard: "Bart Bucks" are not legal tender.

Couch: Homer arrives first and lies on the couch, then the others sit on him.

Saturdays of Thunder (8F07) 14 November 1991

Homer helps Bart build a soapbox racer hoping to build up their relationship. Bart is easily beaten by Martin's aerodynamically superior machine, but when Martin is injured during time trials, Bart has to decide whether to be Martin's replacement driver, or race in his soapbox and lose to Nelson.

Blackboard: I will not fake rabies(this didn't appear in the original USA airings).

Couch: The seat cushions have disappeared and the family falls into the couch.

Flaming Moe's (8F08) 21 November 1991

Homer invents the hottest drink in Springfield the 'Flaming Homer'. Moe steals the recipe, names it the 'Flaming Moe' and turns his Tavern into the place to be in Springfield. A chain of bars, Tipsy McStagger's, offers Moe a million dollars for the recipe, but Moe's chance for great wealth is about to be spoiled by a vengeful Homer.

Guest Stars: Catherine O'Hara and Aerosmith.

Blackboard: Underwear should be worn on the inside (has anyone told Radioactive Man?).

Couch: As everybody sits two burglars, who are holding the couch, tip them off and carry the couch away.

Phone Call For: Uh, Hugh Jass? Oh, somebody check the men's room for a Hugh Jass!

Burns Verkaufen der Kraftwerk (Burns Sells The Power Plant) (8F09) 5 December 1991

Homer loses his job as 'safety inspector' when Mr. Burns sells the Springfield Nuclear Power Plant to German businessmen for $100,000,000. While they find the 'hidden extras' in the plant, a confrontation in Moe's with a drunken Homer shows Monty Burns that without his position of power he is no longer feared.

Blackboard: The Christmas Pageant does not stink.

Couch: Santa's Little Helper is on the couch snarling and keeps the family off it.

Phone Call For: Bea O'Problem! Bea O'Problem! Come on, guys, do I have a Bea O'Problem here?

I Married Marge (8F10) 5 December 1991

The sequel to *The Way We Was.* It's 1980. After a romantic visit to see *The Empire Strikes Back* and its aftermath Marge finds she is pregnant with Bart. Homer is determined to do right by her, proposes and tries to provide for them and their child. But everything seems to go wrong...

Blackboard: I will not torment the emotionally frail.

Couch: The family cartwheels to the couch, except for Maggie who hops there, and strikes an open arm flourish.

Radio Bart (8F11) 9 January 1992

For his tenth birthday Bart receives a radio microphone, which he promptly uses to play practical jokes on everyone. He convinces Springfield that a little boy named Timmy O'Toole has fallen down a local well, but events turn against him when he himself falls down the well.

Guest Stars: Sting as himself, fronting a parody of Live Aid's *We Are the World* titled *We're Sending Our Love Down The Well.*

Blackboard: I will not carve gods.

Couch: The family bounces up and down on the couch changing position with each bounce.

Lisa the Greek (8F12) 23 January 1992

Lisa forges a closer relationship with Homer when he discovers her football predicting skills. As Super Bowl approaches Lisa realises that the relationship may end until next year's football season. (repeats of this episode had portions redubbed for later Super Bowls.)

Couch: Homer sits on Santa's Little Helper then pulls him out from beneath him.

Homer at the Bat (8F13) 20 February 1992

Mr. Burns replaces his power plant's Softball team with ringers (including Roger Clemens, Wade Boggs, Ken Griffey Jr., Steve Sax, Don Mattingly, Ozzie Smith, Darryl Strawberry, Jose Canseco and Mike Scoscia) to win a $1,000,000 bet that they can beat the Shelbyville plant's team. The day before the match all of the ringers are injured in freak accidents leaving the real team members to win the day.

Guest Stars: The above plus Terry Cashman.

Blackboard: I will not aim for the head.

Couch: The family rushes in, and with the sole exception of Maggie, bang their heads together and collapse unconscious on the floor.

Homer Alone (8F14) 6 February 1992

Driven to the edge of her sanity by the dysfunctional horrorshow that is her family, Marge takes a vacation at Rancho Relaxo. She leaves Lisa and Bart with Patty and Selma, and Homer alone with Maggie. In the night Maggie goes searching for Marge.

Blackboard: I will not spank others.

Couch: Everybody forms a pyramid.

Separate Vocations (8F15) February 27, 1992

The disappointing results of the Career Aptitude Normalisation Test, (or CANT) find Lisa is suited to be a homemaker, while Bart would be an ideal police officer. While Bart becomes the most efficient hall monitor Principal Skinner has ever had, Lisa becomes a Brandoesque rebel.

Guest Stars: Steve Allen.

Blackboard: I will not barf unless I'm sick/I will not expose the ignorance of the faculty.

Couch: Bart lands across everyone's lap.

Bart the Lover (8F16) 13 February 1992

Infuriated at being kept in detention by Edna Krabappel, Bart discovers she has placed a personal ad and he responds in the name of Woodrow. Soon he has built the romance up to the point where Edna is devastated by Woodrow's no-show at their first date. How will Bart resolve this 'romance'?

Couch: An alien disappears through a trap door in the floor just before the family appears.

What's been cut? Two bits of near swearing by the BBC. Homer in church nearly gets to say 'damn' ('da – ' in the episode) and later manages half a 'bastard' while talking to Flanders about his commercial work. Both left intact by SKY.

Dog of Death (8F17) 12 March 1992

The Simpsons have to sacrifice their favourite things to raise money for Santa's Little Helper to have an operation for his twisted stomach. After the operation they take their frustrations at their reduced lifestyle out on the poor dog, which wanders off , eventually becoming one of Mr. Burns' hounds.

Blackboard: I saw nothing unusual in the teacher's lounge.

Couch: Homer arrives first and lies on the couch, then the others sit on him.

Colonel Homer (8F19) 26 March 1992

After embarrassing Marge at the movies, Homer drives to a bar where he discovers a country singer named Lurleen Lumpkin. He becomes her manager, Colonel Homer, to Marge's disgust.

Guest Stars: Beverly D'Angelo.

Blackboard: I will not conduct my own fire drills.

Couch: The seat cushions have disappeared and the family falls into the couch.

Black Widower (8F20) 9 April 1992

Sideshow Bob is paroled, and after a whirlwind romance marries Selma. Bart suspects that Sideshow Bob has something on his mind other than matrimony, and when the Simpsons receive a video of the honeymoon his suspicions are confirmed.

Guest Stars: Kelsey Grammer.

Blackboard: Funny noises are not funny.

Couch: As everybody sits two burglars, who are holding the couch, tip them off and carry the couch away.

The Otto Show (8F21) 23 April 1992

After losing his job driving the school bus because he doesn't have a driver's license, Otto is kicked out of his apartment and ends up living with the Simpsons. Homer finds living with a bigger slob than himself trying, and Otto has to try to get himself a driving license.

Guest Stars: Spinal Tap.

Blackboard: I will not spin the turtle.

Couch: Santa's Little Helper is on the couch snarling and keeps the family off it.

Bart's Friend Falls In Love (8F22) 7 May 1992

Bart is appalled to find that Milhouse has gone soft when Milhouse dates a new girl... without her father knowing it. Meanwhile, Homer tries to lose weight by listening to a subliminal tape.

Guest Stars: Kimmy Robertson

Blackboard: I will not snap bras.

Couch: The couch tips over backwards, and everybody crashes through the back wall.

Brother, Can You Spare Two Dimes? (8F23) 27 August 1992

Herbert Powell (*Oh Brother, Where Art Thou?*) returns, and asks Homer to help him with an invention idea of his, using the $2,000 Homer received from the nuclear plant for 'Outstanding Achievement in the Field of Excellence' (in fact a Burns scam to get Homer to sign a waiver absolving Burns from any responsibility in the matter of Homer's damaged sperm count).

Guest Stars: Joe Frazier and Danny DeVito.

Blackboard: I will not fake seizures.

Couch: The family cartwheels to the couch, except for Maggie who hops there, and strikes an open arm flourish.

What's been cut?: The BBC cut a load of references to shooting in its first showing of this episode, including (sensitively!) the 'I shot JR' line that emanates from the TV! In addition Bart's wish to use the $2,000 dollars to buy a machine gun and Herb's gift of a membership to the NRA were cut. They've since been reinstated, basically because they don't really make a lot of sense.

Season Four (1992-1993)

Kamp Krusty (8F24) 24 September 1992

To get a Bart-free summer Homer accepts Bart's doctored report card and sends Bart and Lisa to Kamp Krusty. The camp is run along concentration camp rather than summer camp lines, and Bart organises a revolt that leads him to Tijuana with Krusty.

Blackboard: This punishment is not boring and pointless.

Couch: The Simpsons rush in and stop: the couch is occupied by the Flintstones!

What's been cut?: At the closing credits one of the 'photos', featuring Bart and Lisa watching a cockfight has been cut by the BBC.

A Streetcar Named Marge (8F18) 1 October 1992

Marge takes the part of Blanche DuBois against Ned Flanders' Stanley Kowalski in the musical version of *A Streetcar Named Desire*. She finds the anger she needs to play Blanche in her anger with Homer's lack of support for her. Meanwhile Maggie, temporarily abandoned to a day-care centre, leads a revolt against the confiscation of pacifiers (that's dummies to Brits!).

The production company that animates *The Simpsons* changes from Klasky-Csupo to Film Roman – Klasky-Csupo go on to great success with *Rugrats* (amongst others).

Blackboard: My name is not Dr. Death.

Couch: The couch swallows The Simpsons as it transforms into a monster.

Homer the Heretic (9F01) 8 October 1992

Having had an ideal Sunday avoiding church, Homer vows not to go again: in a dream God sanctions his decision. The next Sunday he stays home against Marge's objections. She is certain something terrible will happen. And she's right.

Blackboard: I will not defame New Orleans (New Orleans complained about the opening song in *Oh, Streetcar*!). Originally shown with no board.

Couch: The family rushes in, sits down and disappears as the couch rotates 180 degrees into a secret door in the wall and is replaced by an empty couch.

Lisa the Beauty Queen (9F02) 15 October 1992

Noticing that Lisa isn't confident about her looks, Homer sells his prize ticket for a trip on the Duff blimp to finance Lisa's entry into the Little Miss Springfield contest. Lisa comes in as runner up, but when the original winner is injured Lisa ascends to the crown, and becomes the spokeschild for the sponsor Laramie Cigarettes, which she promptly denounces from their float as evil.

Guest Stars: Bob Hope.

Blackboard: I will not prescribe medication. Originally shown with the blackboard message from *Homer the Heretic.*

Couch: Maggie is already seated, Homer, Marge, and Bart sprint to the edge of the film, back into frame and onto the couch.

Itchy & Scratchy: The Movie (9F03) 3 November 1992

When Bart babysitting Maggie results in her driving the family car into Springfield State Penitentiary, Homer takes a draconian measure against Bart's troublemaking: Bart can never see *The Itchy and Scratchy Movie*.

Blackboard: I will not bury the new kid.

Couch: The Simpsons sit on the couch, which deflates as if filled with air.

What's been cut?: It's easier to say what hasn't. At various times SKY and the BBC have both had their hands on this episode. Here we go...

The BBC cut the scene where Edna Krabappel talks about Bart to Marge. Before she says: "Bart has been guilty of the following atrocities..." she pulls a Krusty doll out of her desk drawer and shows it to Marge, pulling the head off to reveal a machete-blade. The sequence with the doll has been cut. Later when Homer says to Bart "Someday you'll thank me for this son." Bart replies "Not bloody likely!" You can guess what has been cut.

On SKY the following cuts were made:

a) In the trailer for *The Itchy & Scratchy Movie*, after Itchy waits for Scratchy to reach the rotating blade on the conveyor belt he grabs an axe and chops Scratchy into little pieces with it.

b) A complete scene has been cut after Homer watches the Bumblebee man on TV, and before he catches Bart smashing the mustard packets. We see a billboard for the Movie spurting blood over a newlywed couple driving past in a convertible.

c) In the 'Steamboat Itchy' short, after Itchy kneecaps Scratchy, Scratchy is trapped in a furnace, where he writhes in agony as he burns. Itchy then opens the grate and pulls out Scratchy's burnt head:

ITCHY – "Oh me, Oh my!"

d) In the 'World War II' short, after Itchy and Scratchy start bashing Hitler with their implements we see Itchy decapitate Hitler with an axe, then shake hands with Scratchy. Itchy then decapitates Scratchy too. The music changes from *Stars and Stripes Forever* to *Happy Days Are Here Again* and a cartoon Roosevelt dances on and kicks the carcasses of Hitler and Scratchy. Itchy holds up a 'Save Scrap Iron' sign.

e) Another small scene cut. After the shots of the cinema showing *The Itchy & Scratchy Movie* coming to the end of its run, there's another shot of the blood-spurting Itchy & Scratchy billboard, which now advertises Springfield Barber College.

Treehouse of Horror III (9F04) 29 October 1992

The Simpsons hold a Halloween Party where three stories are told:

Clown Without Pity

Bart's birthday present is a talking Krusty doll... from House of Evil – 'Your One Stop Evil Shop'. The doll promptly starts to stalk Homer, until a repairman finds a Good/Evil switch on its back. A parody of the *Living Doll* episode of *The Twilight Zone*, among other 'doll of evil' classics.

King Homer

A King Kong Klone, with our hero, Homer, as the giant ape.

Dial 'Z' For Zombies

After finding a book in the library that explains how to bring the dead to life, Bart tries to raise the dead Snowball I, but instead causes every dead person in Springfield to reanimate. A parody of Stephen King's *Pet Sematary* crossed with *Night Of The Living Dead.*

Couch: The family's skeletons rush in and sit on the couch. Marge's skeleton has hair with a *Bride of Frankenstein* streak in it.

Marge Gets a Job (9F05) 5 November 1992

After Homer's stupidity results in his house needing about $8,000 worth of foundation work, Marge gets a job at the Springfield Nuclear Power Plant and Mr Burns develops a crush on Marge. While Mr Burns enlists Smithers' help in kidnapping Tom Jones to ensure Marge's undying love, Bart learns not to cry wolf the hard way – when a real wolf enters the school.

Guest Stars: Tom Jones.

Blackboard: I will not teach others to fly.

Couch: The Simpsons enter with each other's heads. They remove them and switch until they have the right heads.

New Kid on the Block (9F06) 12 November 1992

Bart falls for Laura Powers, the new girl next door, when she babysits for him. When she dates Jimbo, Bart plans to help her see Jimbo's true nature. Meanwhile Homer is ejected from the Frying Dutchman on an 'all you can eat' night and seeks legal redress.

Guest Stars: Sara Gilbert (Darlene from *Roseanne*).

Blackboard: I will not bring sheep to class.

Couch: The couch falls through the floor.

Phone Call For: Uh, Amanda Huggenkiss? Hey, I'm looking for Amanda Huggenkiss! Ah, why can't I find Amanda Huggenkiss? *And:* Ivana Tinkle? Ivana Tinkle? All right, everybody, put down your glasses, Ivana Tinkle!

Mr. Plow (9F07) 19 November 1992

Homer buys a snowplow after wrecking the two family cars during a snowstorm, and starts up in business as Mr. Plow, enjoying success and stimulating Marge's libido. The competition becomes cut-throat when Barney starts up business as Plow King.

Guest Stars: Linda Ronstadt and Adam West.

Blackboard: A burp is not an answer.

Couch: A wooden chair has been substituted for the couch; the adults share it and the kids sit on their laps.

What's been cut?: The BBC cut a reference to lepers from the 'Carnival of Stars' in the first scene.

Lisa's First Words (9F08) 3 December 1992

When trying to get Maggie to say her first words (receiving a burp in response) Homer recalls Lisa's birth, their move to their current home, and what Lisa said her for her first words. One of the occasional episodes that give us a glimpse into Simpson prehistory.

Blackboard: See below...

Couch: The Simpsons form a chorus line, and are joined by the Rockettes, circus animals, jugglers, trapeze artists, magicians, fire breathers and Santa's Little Helper (amongst others) for a musical spectacular. The most over-the-top couch gag ever, and hence one of the most often re-used.

What's been cut?: The blackboard gag *Teacher is not a leper* has been replaced with *I will not teach others to fly* from *Maggie Gets a Job* by the leper-friendly BBC.

Homer's Triple Bypass (9F09) 17 December 1992

Homer's years of eating fatty foods have brought on a heart attack, and he is forced to have a bypass operation. His choice: $40,000 for Dr. Hibbert or $129.95 for Dr. Nick Riviera! Luckily a junior Simpson has been reading up on bypass surgery.

Blackboard: Coffee is not for kids (a message that becomes shakier and less legible as it makes its way down the board).

Couch: A tiny Simpsons family rushes in and starts to climb the giant couch; Maggie has to be pulled up.

Marge vs. the Monorail (9F10) 17 December 1992

The town has fined Montgomery Burns three million dollars for his illegal disposal of nuclear waste. Now they have to decide what to spend the money on. Predictably enough they buy a needless monorail from a used monorail salesman, and Marge has to enlist the help of Leonard Nimoy to avert disaster.

Guest Stars: Leonard Nimoy.

Blackboard: I will not eat things for money.

Couch: The Simpsons rush in and sit, just before the room is filled with what seems like most of Springfield.

Selma's Choice (9F11) 21 January 1993

The death of her childless Aunt, Gladys Bouvier, convinces Selma to try and get married and have a child. She is on the point of considering sperm donation when a sick Homer causes Marge to ask Selma to look after the kids on a day out to Duff Gardens.

Blackboard: I will not yell "She's Dead" during roll call.

Couch: The family rushes in, sits down and disappears as the couch rotates 180 degrees into a secret door in the wall and is replaced by an empty couch.

Brother from the Same Planet (9F12) 4 February 1993

When Homer forgets to pick him up after soccer practise, Bart joins the Bigger Brother program, which offers adult male role models to boys without them. Rejected, Homer joins the program as a Big Brother. Meanwhile, Lisa is addicted to the premium charging Corey hot line.

Blackboard: The principal's toupee is not a Frisbee.

Couch: Before they reach the couch the Simpsons are caught and hoisted into the air by a hunter's net spread on the floor.

I Love Lisa (9F13) 11 February 1993

Lisa's sympathy for the mentally subnormal Ralph Wiggum causes him to think that she is his girlfriend. The expected rejection fuels his performance in the school play, astounding the audience with his thespian abilities.

Blackboard: I will not call the principal "spud head".

Couch: The Simpsons form a chorus line, and are joined by the Rockettes, circus animals, jugglers, trapeze artists, magicians, fire breathers and Santa's Little Helper (amongst others) for a musical spectacular.

Duffless (9F14) 18 February 1993

After Homer gets caught drunk driving, he promises Marge to stay off the Duff for one month. Meanwhile, when Bart ruins Lisa's science project, Lisa vows to take revenge by determining which is smarter: a hamster or Bart.

Blackboard: Goldfish don't bounce.

Couch: Maggie is already seated, Homer, Marge, and Bart sprint to the edge of the film, back into frame and onto the couch.

What's been cut?: The BBC cut a complete scene, after Homer jumps out of the power plant window.

Outside the plant Barney is waiting for Homer in his car. A mattress is tied to the roof to cushion Homer's fall.

BARNEY – "Hey! That looks like Princess Di. (He drives forward a few feet. Homer hits the ground behind the car.) Aw, wait, it's just a pile of rags."

A shot of Skinner's buttocks (just prior to Bart throwing a tomato at them) was also cut, but later restored.

Last Exit to Springfield (9F15) 18 February 1993

Homer becomes a Union boss and negotiates a new contract with the Springfield Nuclear Power Plant, mindful that Lisa needs braces.

Guest Stars: Dr. Joyce Brothers.

Blackboard: Mud is not one of the 4 food groups.

Couch: The couch swallows The Simpsons as it transforms into a monster.

So It's Come to This: A Simpsons Clip Show (9F17) 1 April 1993

Homer is injured when Bart's April Fools joke (a can of Duff shaken to extremes and planted in the fridge) works better than expected. At the hospital the Simpsons recall various moments from past episodes.

Blackboard: No one is interested in my underpants.

Couch: The Simpsons enter with each other's heads. They remove them and switch until they have the right heads.

The Front (9F16) 15 April 1993

After suffering through a particularly lame Itchy and Scratchy episode, Lisa and Bart write their own, but find no-one will take them seriously. When they submit it using their grandfather's name they become top I&S scriptwriters. Meanwhile, Homer attends night school to make up a missing science credit.

Guest Stars: Brooke Shields and David Crosby.

Blackboard: I will not sell miracle cures.

Couch: The Simpsons form a chorus line, and are joined by the Rockettes, circus animals, jugglers, trapeze artists, magicians, fire breathers and Santa's Little Helper (amongst others) for a musical spectacular.

Whacking Day (9F18) 29 April 1993

Lisa dreads the onset of Whacking Day, where the citizens of Springfield kill snakes by whacking them to death with stick and Bart is expelled from school for embarrassing Mr. Skinner during a school inspection.

Guest Stars: Barry White.

Blackboard: I will return the seeing-eye dog.

Couch: A wooden chair has been substituted for the couch; the adults share it and the kids sit on their laps.

Krusty Gets Kancelled (9F19) 13 May 1993

The runaway popularity of the Gabbo show gets Krusty cancelled. On the skids, Krusty is helped by Lisa and Bart who organise a comeback special.

Guest Stars: Bette Midler, Elizabeth Taylor, Hugh Hefner, Johnny Carson, Luke Perry and The Red Hot Chili Peppers.

Blackboard: I will not charge admission to the bathroom.

Couch: Before they reach the couch the Simpsons are caught and hoisted into the air by a hunter's net spread on the floor.

Marge in Chains (9F20) 6 May 1993

Suffering from Osaka Flu Marge accidentally shoplifts from the Kwik-E-Mart and has to spend 30 days in the Springfield prison.

Blackboard: I do not have diplomatic immunity.

Couch: A tiny Simpsons family rushes in and starts to climb the giant couch; Maggie has to be pulled up.

Season Five (1993-1994)

Homer's Barbershop Quartet (9F21) 30 September 1993

A flashback episode (to 1985) with Homer, Apu, Principal Skinner, and Chief Wiggum (later replaced with Barney) as the hit barbershop quartet the 'B Sharps'.

Guest Stars: George Harrison.

Blackboard: I will never win an Emmy (This was the first time the show became eligible for "Best Comedy Series", but wasn't nominated).

Couch: The family runs into each other and shatters on the floor; Santa's Little Helper examines the damage. Then they run into each other and end up on the couch as a five-headed 'blob'. Finally they run into each other and explode. Maggie's pacifier drops to the ground. These have subsequently been used as separate couch gags for other episodes.

Cape Feare (9F22) 7 October 1993

When Sideshow Bob is paroled from prison the Simpsons are enrolled in a Witness Protection Program as 'The Thompsons', and are moved from Springfield to the inauspiciously named Cape Feare. But Bob has followed them, and he has only one thing in mind for Bart: revenge.

Guest Stars: Kelsey Grammer.

Blackboard: The cafeteria deep fryer is not a toy.

Couch: The Simpsons form a chorus line, and are joined by the Rockettes, circus animals, jugglers, trapeze artists, magicians, fire breathers and Santa's Little Helper (amongst others) for a musical spectacular.

Rosebud (1F01) 21 October 1993

In a flashback to the early years of Montgomery Burns (a clever parody of *Citizen Kane*) we see him abandon his teddy bear, Bobo, for a life of riches. In his dotage he wants Bobo back, but Bobo has passed into the ownership of Maggie Simpson...

Guest Stars: The Ramones.

Couch: The family stops: the couch is already occupied by a family of Simpson doppelgangers.

What's been cut?: Both SKY and the BBC cut the Ramones calling Monty Burns an 'old bastard', but only SKY cut Selma's 'Holy Crap' and Burns' reference to 'paparazzi', although the latter (made in deference to Princess Diana's death) was restored.

Homer Goes to College (1F02) 14 October 1993

Due to the plant failing a safety inspection Monty Burns is told that he must get Homer up to speed or legal action will be taken. Homer's job and the future of his family hinges on his successful completion of Nuclear Physics 101.

Couch: The Simpsons sit down to be crushed by a giant foot from Monty Python's Flying Circus.

Treehouse of Horror IV (1F04) 28 October 1993

From a hall of paintings reminiscent of *Night Gallery*, Bart presents three tales of terror...

The Devil and Homer Simpson

Homer gives up his soul for a single donut. Now, the Devil wants Homer.

Terror at 5½ Feet

Bart Simpson has a nightmare about a bus crash. And his nightmare is about to come true when a playful gremlin starts taking the bus apart piece by piece.

Bart Simpson's Dracula

In a frighteningly accurate parody of Francis Ford Coppola's *Dracula*, Monty Burns is a vampire out for the blood of Bart and the rest of the Simpsons.

What's been cut?: SKY cut a 'bastard' from Homer's dialogue. The BBC cut a section from Flanders introducing the 'Jury of the Damned' where Richard Nixon protests that he's not dead yet. Of course by the time the BBC showed the episode he was...

Couch: The Simpsons sit down to be crushed by a giant foot from Monty Python's Flying Circus.

Marge on the Lam (1F03) 4 November 1993

When Homer stands her up, Marge goes to the ballet with Ruth Powers, her next door neighbour (mother of Laura, the object of Bart's affections). The next night Ruth takes Marge out – in a stolen car. Suddenly Marge finds herself in the middle of a *Thelma and Louise* parody.

Couch: The couch is painted on a wall, in a Road-runner style, which the Simpsons run at and through, leaving their outlines in the wall.

Bart's Inner Child (1F05) 11 November 1993

When Bart is spotlighted as the embodiment of the 'inner child' by a feel-good therapist, the entire town of Springfield emulates him. This is *not* a good thing...

Guest Stars: James Brown.

Couch: A fat man is occupying most of the couch; The Simpsons squeeze into what room remains.

What's been cut?: Several car crashes and references to royalty were cut by SKY in the wake of Diana's death but later restored.

Boy-Scoutz N The Hood (1F06) 18 November 1993

Bart and Milhouse find $20 and spend it on a pure syrup super-squishy, which results in a squishy-fuelled night of abandon. Bart wakes up to find that he has joined the Junior Campers, a Boy Scouts type organisation. Worse, the den father is Ned Flanders, and Bart and Homer end up on the rafting trip from hell.

Guest Stars: Ernest Borgnine.

Couch: Five pairs of eyes enter in the dark and go to the couch. The light comes on to reveal only the Simpsons' eyes have appeared, as five eyeless bodies quickly enter, sit down, and pop their eyes into their sockets.

The Last Temptation of Homer (1F07) 9 December 1993

Homer finds himself attracted to Mindy, a new female employee at the nuclear plant who in all respects except for looks is his female doppelganger. When Mindy and Homer are sent to the National Energy Convention in Capital City together Homer fears he may succumb to temptation... Meanwhile corrective medical measures leave Bart looking and sounding like a nerd.

Guest Stars: Michelle Pfeiffer and Werner Klemperer.

Blackboard: All work and no play makes Bart a dull boy.

Couch: The family sits and belatedly notice that the couch is on the set of David Letterman's show as Dave swings his chair around to face forward.

What's been cut?: A 'bastard' by both SKY and the BBC, spoken by Homer at the National Energy Convention.

$pringfield (or, How I Learned To Stop Worrying And Love Legalised Gambling) (1F08) 16 December 1993

When the local economy stalls, everyone, including Marge, votes to legalise gambling in Springfield. Mr. Burns even opens up his own casino, Homer gets to be a blackjack dealer, and Marge is addicted to the slot machines.

Guest Stars: Gerry Cooney and Robert Goulet.

Blackboard: I will not say "Springfield" just to get applause.

Homer the Vigilante (1F09) 6 January 1994

When a cat burglar hits Springfield, Homer ends up leading the Neighbourhood Watch, a group who are more dangerous to Springfield than the burglar. Meanwhile Grandpa has his eyes on a new resident at the retirement home.

Guest Stars: Sam Neill.

Blackboard: I am not authorised to fire substitute teachers.

What's been cut?: At the vigilante group meeting, where the vigilantes all fire their guns by accident the punch line is Bart firing his. Cut by the BBC.

Homer and Apu (1F10) 10 February 1994

Homer gets food poisoning from eating the Kwik-E-Mart food and gets Apu fired. Apu dedicates himself to becoming Homer's personal valet as reparation and Homer vows to get Apu his job back. The new Kwik-E-Mart manager? James Woods.

Guest Stars: James Woods.

Blackboard: I will not go near the kindergarten turtle.

Couch: The Simpsons poke their head up one by one from behind the couch (Maggie does it from behind the centre cushion on the couch).

Bart Gets Famous (1F11) 3 February 1994

Playing truant from a field trip to a cardboard factory, Bart sneaks into the Krusty the Clown show, and becomes his assistant. When Bart accidentally wrecks a set on live TV and utters 'I didn't do it' he is launched into instant stardom as the 'I didn't do it' boy. But fame is fleeting…

Guest Stars: Former Simpsons writer/producer Conan O'Brien as himself on his chat show.

Blackboard: My homework was not stolen by a one-armed man (a reference to long-running TV series *The Fugitive*).

Lisa vs. Malibu Stacy (1F12) 3 February 1994

Lisa buys a Malibu Stacy doll when Grandpa decides to distribute his estate before he croaks and finds that the doll can only parrot vacuous phrases that demean women. Lisa finds Stacy Lovell, the creator of the doll, and they produce Lisa Lionheart, a new doll that embodies the qualities they admire in women.

Guest Stars: Kathleen Turner.

Deep Space Homer (1F13) 24 February 1994

Facing cancellation because of falling ratings, NASA decides to send a 'blue-collar slob' into space. The race for the first blue-collar slob to venture into space comes down to a two-slob race: Homer Simpson and Barney.

Guest Stars: James Taylor and Buzz Aldrin.

Couch: A fat man is occupying most of the couch; The Simpsons squeeze into what room remains.

Homer Loves Flanders (1F14) 17 March 1994

When Ned Flanders provides Homer with a ticket to a sold-out football game Homer becomes his best friend. Shortly afterwards Ned develops a pathological hatred of Homer...

Blackboard: I am not delightfully saucy.

Couch: The family rush in and see two couches. They then each split into two halves, taking a seat on each couch.

Bart Gets An Elephant (1F15) 31 March 1994

When Bart has the choice of $10,000 or an African Elephant, KBBL is taken off guard when Bart wants the elephant and eventually have to cough one up. Stampy, as he becomes known, eats the Simpsons out of house and home and shares profound destructive tendencies with his juvenile owner. Before Homer can sell Stampy to an ivory dealer Bart sets him free.

Introducing: Cletus, the slack jawed yokel.

Blackboard: Organ transplants are best left to the professionals.

Couch: Five pairs of eyes enter in the dark and go to the couch. The light comes on to reveal only the Simpsons' eyes have appeared, as five eyeless bodies quickly enter, sit down, and pop their eyes into their sockets.

Burns' Heir (1F16) 14 April 1994

A brush with death in the form of a near drowning in his bathtub convinces Monty Burns that he must find an heir. When Bart vandalises Burns' mansion his malevolence convinces Monty he's found his successor. Bart stays at Maison Burns, where his doting 'father' caters for his every whim.

Blackboard: The Pledge of Allegiance does not end with Hail Satan.

Couch: The family bounce into the living room shaped as balls and bounce around before landing on the couch and resuming their normal shape.

What's been cut?: SKY belatedly decided to cut Homer saying 'crap' sometime in the late 1990s.

Sweet Seymour Skinner's Baddasssss Song (1F18) 27 April 1994

Bart brings Santa's Little Helper to school for Show and Tell, and he promptly crawls into the heating ducts, leading to Principal Skinner being fired by Superintendent Chalmers. Ned Flanders becomes the new head and Bart has to scheme to get Skinner back. This is the 100th episode of the series.

Blackboard: I will not celebrate meaningless milestones.

Couch: The family rush in and sit, then Homer gets up, rips the FOX logo from the screen corner, and they all stomp on it.

The Boy Who Knew Too Much (1F19) 5 May 1994

When Bart skips class he witnesses a waiter brutally beaten at Freddy Quimby's birthday party. Freddy is blamed and is prosecuted, but Bart can clear him – if he's willing to risk the wrath of Principal Skinner for truanting.

Blackboard: There are plenty of businesses like show business.

Couch: The family sits and belatedly notice that the couch is on the set of David Letterman's show as Dave swings his chair around to face forward.

What's been cut?: SKY cut some mild swearing, and the first appearance of the 'L'il Bastard' products which finally appear in *The Joy Of Sect.* Unfortunately this destroys one of the jokes.

Secrets of a Successful Marriage (1F20) 19 May 1994

Worrying about being slow, Homer enrols in an adult education class and ends up teaching a marriage course. He only succeeds as a teacher when he starts to tell the class about some of Marge's bedroom secrets.

Blackboard: Five days is not too long to wait for a gun.

What's been cut?: More swearing by SKY.

Lady Bouvier's Lover (1F21) 12 May 1994

Grandpa Simpson falls in love with Jackie, Marge's mother but loses her to the smooth talking Montgomery Burns. When he learns Jackie is going to marry Burns, Grandpa is broken hearted.

Blackboard: I will not re-transmit without the express permission of

Major League Baseball.

What's been cut?: SKY cut Smithers guessing that Monty Burns "...had sex with that old woman?" and some mild swearing.

Season Six (1994-1995)

Bart of Darkness (1F22) 4 September1994

After he breaks his leg, Bart finds himself in an ongoing *Rear Window* situation, spying on the neighbours with a telescope from his bedroom window. Bart finds his view considerably more interesting when he sees Ned Flanders digging what appears to be a grave for his wife.

Blackboard: Beans are neither fruit nor musical.

Couch: The family sits on an invisible couch. The couch enters in pieces and forms itself on top of them, causing them to fall to the floor.

What's been cut?: SKY cut various death/royalty references in the wake of Diana's death, all now restored.

Lisa's Rival (1F17) 11 September 1994

Lisa is out-poindextered by Alison, a new student who's smarter, younger, and a better saxophonist than she is. With the school's diorama contest looming will Lisa resort to dirty tricks to regain her position? Meanwhile, Homer turns 'Scarface' as he corners the market in a certain white powder when a sugar truck overturns.

Guest Stars: Winona Ryder.

Blackboard: No one is interested in my underpants, the same as *So It's Come to This: A Simpsons Clip Show.*

Couch: The couch floats on water with only the tops of the Simpsons' heads visible until they reach it (Bart uses a snorkel).

What's been cut?: SKY made a cut purely to shorten the episode; when Lisa faints at the audition she first wakes up to be told that Alison has won. She faints again, and comes to, thinking that her first period of consciousness was a dream. She finds that it's not. SKY have cut the first awakening, robbing the succeeding dialogue of much of its humour (not to mention sense!).

Another Simpsons Clip Show (2F33) 25 September 1994

The Bridges of Madison County prompts Marge and Homer to try to teach the kids about romance. Cue clips from 28 past episodes.

Blackboard: I will not use abbrev.

Itchy & Scratchy Land (2F01) 2 October 1994

Bart and Lisa persuade Marge and Homer to take them to Itchy &

Scratchy Land, "the violentest place on earth," a holiday destination reminiscent of *Westworld* in more ways than one. Demented animatronic Itchy and Scratchy robots in hunted yellow people shocker!

Blackboard: I am not the reincarnation of Sammy Davis Jr.

Couch: The Simpsons materialise on the couch in original Star Trek style.

What's been cut?: SKY cut the 'L'il Bastard Travelling Kit'.

Sideshow Bob Roberts (2F02) 9 October 1994

Right-wing radio talk show host Birch Barlow helps persuade Mayor Quimby to release Sideshow Bob from prison. Once released Bob runs against the mayor, wins, and begins to build the Matlock Expressway through the Simpsons' house. Bart and Lisa (with the help of 'Deep Throat' Waylon Smithers) set out to prove Bob's victory was faked.

Guest Stars: Kelsey Grammer.

Couch: Five pairs of eyes enter in the dark and go to the couch. The light comes on to reveal only the Simpsons' eyes have appeared, as five eyeless bodies quickly enter, sit down, and pop their eyes into their sockets.

Treehouse of Horror V (2F03) 30 October 1994

In an *Outer Limits* parody, the Simpsons control the vertical, the horizontal, and everything else come to that, in the terror and foul horror that is Treehouse V...

The Shinning

In a parody of Stephen King's *The Shining*, lack of TV and beer drives Homer into homicidal insanity at the mountain lodge where he has become caretaker for the winter. Only Bart's 'shinning' can save the family.

Time and Punishment

A loose parody of Ray Bradbury's *A Sound of Thunder*, where Homer finds Ned Flanders as the ruler of an Orwellian world when he inadvertently changes the past. Returning to the past again and again Homer only makes the present world worse, until he finally settles for a 'best fit.'

Nightmare Cafeteria

A grotesque version of *Soylent Green* is presented when Bart and Lisa find out how Principal Skinner has solved the double bind of overcrowding at the school and budget cuts in the cafeteria...

Guest Stars: James Earl Jones.

Couch: Ghoulish Simpsons enter with mismatched body parts – Lisa has one of Bart's legs for her right arm, and so on. When they sit on the couch they pass around each others parts until they match.

What's been cut?: This is one of the most butchered episodes ever, and I'd recommend you try and see it on video or the BBC (if they pass it uncut). On the other hand the Simpsons *Treehouse of Horror* episodes are the only ones to have ever upset my kids, so there you go…

a) In the opening credits shots of Moe's body falling from a tree in a noose and then reanimating and the Reverend Lovejoy burning Patty and Selma at the stake as they use the fire to light their cigarettes, as well as Bart getting decapitated have been cut.

b) In *The Shinning*, various derogatory references to John Denver were cut, but later restored, in the wake of the singer's death.

c) After Homer says "see ya later" in *The Shinning* on his way to the axe collection the following dialogue is cut:

LISA – "Mom, is dad going to kill us?"

MARGE – "We're just going to have to wait and see."

d) An entire scene immediately following the above cut has been removed, with Homer being advised to kill his family as he sits at the bar talking to a spectral Moe.

e) When Homer kills Groundskeeper Willie the shot of the axe embedded in Willie's back has been cut:

WILLIE – "Aw, is that the best you can do?"

f) In *Time and Punishment* Groundskeeper Willie's axing by Maggie is cut, as is a rare speaking part for her (voiced by James Earl Jones):

MAGGIE – "This is indeed a disturbing universe."

g) In *Nightmare Cafeteria* Groundskeeper Willie makes yet another rescue bid, only to be axed. Belatedly he realises:

WILLIE – "Argh! Oh, I'm bad at this."

The 'dying Willie' thread of the episode is completely lost by these cuts, especially as his second death isn't even implied in this version.

h) Again in *Nightmare Cafeteria* a shot of Lunchlady Doris being splattered with Milhouse's blood is cut.

Bart's Girlfriend (2F04) 6 November 1994

Bart's falls in love with the Reverend's Lovejoy's daughter, Jessica. Jessica is attracted by his bad behaviour, and it turns out she is more than his equal in villainy. His romance is short-lived when she steals the church collection plate and he is blamed for it.

Guest Stars: Meryl Streep.

Blackboard: I will not send lard through the mail.

Couch: Five pairs of eyes enter in the dark and go to the couch. The light comes on to reveal only the Simpsons' eyes have appeared, as five eyeless bodies quickly enter, sit down, and pop their eyes into their sockets.

Lisa on Ice (2F05) 13 November 1994

Failing at school because she's bad at sports, Lisa tries to find one that she's good at. She finally finds that ice hockey is ideal – one problem: she's a better hockey player than Bart is. They end up on opposite teams, tied in the big play-off.

Blackboard: I will not dissect things unless instructed.

Couch: The Simpsons are ejected from the couch and get their heads stuck in the ceiling.

Homer: Bad Man (2F06) 27 November 1994

Homer's is accused of sexual harassment by baby-sitter Ashley Grant when his lust for candy leads him to make a grab for a piece that is stuck to her rear. He is pilloried in the media and his life becomes a nightmare from which he will only be released by Groundskeeper Willie and his strange 'hobby'.

Guest Stars: Dennis Franz.

Blackboard: I will not whittle hall passes out of soap.

Couch: The Simpsons have to chase the couch as it and the wall back away from them.

What's been cut?: SKY cuts: as well as some swearing a shot of 'Homer' (in the *Portrait Of an Ass-Grabber* film) running over a cat has been cut. When Groundskeeper Willie runs the videotape that proves Homer's innocence, the first section of it shows Mayor Quimby having sex. This (unsurprisingly) has been cut.

Grandpa vs. Sexual Inadequacy (2F07) 4 December 1994

Homer and Marge's sex life has dwindled to nothing when Grandpa Simpson's helps revive it with his home-made love tonic. Marge suggests they go into business selling it, and father and son take to the road, selling it town to town. Unfortunately forced proximity is bad for the bond between Father and Son. Meanwhile, the increase in adult sexual activity leads Bart to think that aliens have invaded Springfield.

Blackboard: A repeat of 'My homework was not stolen by a one-armed man' from *Bart Gets Famous.*

Couch: The Simpsons run past the same TV and couch again and again, in a Hanna-Barbera cheap animation style, except for Maggie who sits there grinning.

What's been cut?: As with *Treehouse V*, what hasn't... SKY have cut the following:

a) Homer and Marge discussing Homer's performance problems. Marge suggests they could get a book:

HOMER – "Ooh, OK!"

MARGE – "A tasteful book."
HOMER – "Oh, alright."
Only the last line of this exchange is retained.
b) Marge's embarrassment at looking at various Marital Relationship books is compounded when Bart and Lisa appear in the bookshop. In their haste to cover up Marge picks up a book on tanks, Homer s book is of Robert Mapplethorpe's work:
HOMER – "Yes, and I'm pursuing my interest in... (looks at Mapplethorpe book) Aah!!"
c) Homer and Abe talking about sex:
ABE – "What? Seeeeeeeex? What's so unappealing about you and your elderly father talking about sex? I had seeeeeeeex."
(Homer groans.)
d) When Abe gives Homer his tonic:
ABE – "Here you go, you ingrate. Think of me when you're having the best sex of your life."
e) When the tonic works:
Montage of a train running into a tunnel, a rocket taking off, and hot dogs on an assembly line. The camera pulls revealing a movie screen – Bart and Lisa are in the cinema watching this.
LISA – "What do you think Mom and Dad are doing right now?"
BART – "I dunno."
f) Homer referring to the tonic as 'our sex drug' has been cut.
God knows what will happen to episodes like this now the BBC is showing *The Simpsons* as part of its children's anthology programme *Live and Kicking* on a Saturday morning.

Fear of Flying (2F08) 18 December 1994

After Homer's search for booze leads him to nearly fly a commercial aeroplane he is offered free air tickets to avoid bad publicity. Unfortunately it turns out that Marge has a pathological fear of flying, and Marge visits psychiatrist Dr Zweig to find out why she has this problem.

Guest Stars: Anne Bancroft and Ted Danson, Woody Harrelson, Rhea Perlman, John Ratzenberger and George Wendt as the cast of *Cheers*.

Blackboard: Ralph won't "morph" if you squeeze him hard enough.

Couch: The Simpsons form a chorus line, and are joined by the Rockettes, circus animals, jugglers, trapeze artists, magicians, fire breathers and Santa's Little Helper (amongst others) for a musical spectacular.

Homer the Great (2F09) 8 January 1995

Discovering that nearly all his friends belong, Homer joins the secret society of Stonecutters, where his birthmark reveals him to be the true leader of the organisation. At Lisa's suggestion Homer uses his power for the good of the community, and all the other Stonecutters leave to found the Ancient Mystic Society of No Homers.

Guest Stars: Patrick Stewart.

Blackboard: Adding "just kidding" doesn't make it okay to insult the Principal.

Couch: Each of the Simpsons runs to the couch from a different direction in an M.C. Escher version of their house.

And Maggie Makes Three (2F10) 22 January 1995

Lisa wonders why there are no photos of Maggie in the family album. Homer tells the story of how he received a paycheck that let him pay off his debts, insult Monty Burns and take his dream job as a bowling alley attendant. A night of passion with Marge in the flush of his success lead to Maggie and Homer had to relinquish his dream job. The only thing that cheered him up was Maggie, and all her baby photos are on his workstation at the power plant.

Blackboard: "Bagman" is not a legitimate career choice.

Couch: A James Bond style opening, with Homer seen walking in front of the couch framed by a gun barrel. Homer draws his own gun and fires at the camera.

Bart's Comet (2F11) 5 February 1995

Bart's joy when he spots a comet and has it named after him is short-lived when it's discovered that the comet is on a collision course with Springfield. An attempt to blow it to bits with a missile simply destroys the only bridge out of town and now the residents of Springfield must decide who will brave the comet's arrival and who can take refuge in the Ned Flanders' bomb shelter. (Clue: not Ned.) The end of this episode is another *Twilight Zone* clone, from *The Shelter*.

Blackboard: Cursive writing does not mean what I think it does.

Couch: In the style of an early black & white cartoon, The Simpsons wave their hands and do a bow legged bow while wearing Disney style white gloves.

What's been cut?: SKY: Ned Flanders asking for (and getting agreement to) Todd to shoot him if he tries to get back into the shelter.

Homie the Clown (2F12) 12 February 1995

Homer decides to enrol in Krusty's Clown college just as Krusty finds himself pursued by Fat Tony and Co. looking for repayment of his gambling debts. Homer's extraordinary resemblance to his Krustness means the mobsters take him for the real thing.

Guest Stars: Dick Cavett, Joe Mantegna and Johnny Unitas.

Blackboard: Next time it could be me on the scaffolding.

Couch: The family sits on an invisible couch. The couch enters in pieces and forms itself on top of them, causing them to fall to the floor.

What's been cut?: SKY: Lisa using the word 'bastardised'. Oooh!

Bart vs. Australia (2F13) 19 February 1995

When Bart cons an Australian boy into accepting a collect call the government of Australia ends up suing him for fraud. The US state department takes Bart to apologise to the Australian Parliament, but he finds he has also got to take a 'booting' for his crime. A chase ensues which ends with Bart mooning the Australian Prime Minister.

Blackboard: I will not hang donuts on my person.

Couch: The couch floats on water with only the tops of the Simpsons' heads visible until they reach it (Bart uses a snorkel).

What's been cut?: Bad language. For the record two 'bloodies' a 'bum', an 'arse' and a 'crap'.

Homer vs. Patty & Selma (2F14) 26 February 1995

Homer's investment in pumpkin futures goes horribly awry when he fails to sell them before Halloween. The only people who will lend him the money to save himself are Patty and Selma, who make a condition of the load that Homer must wait on them hand and foot. Meanwhile, Bart takes up ballet, when he turns up too late for any of the other PE classes.

Guest Stars: Mel Brooks and Susan Sarandon.

Blackboard: I will remember to take my medication.

Couch: The Simpsons materialise on the couch in original Star Trek style.

A Star is Burns (2F31) 5 March 1995

Marge suggests that a film festival would improve the town's image, and invites Jay 'The Critic' Sherman to guest judge. Monty Burns sees the festival as a way of improving his own image and uses his money to make a big-budget epic, competing against Barney's unexpectedly artistic short and a film by Hans Moleman.

Guest Stars: Jon Lovitz.

Couch: The sizes of the family are reversed as a giant Maggie, down to a tiny Homer, sit on the couch.

What's been cut?: SKY cut the following from 'McBain: Let's Get Silly':

MAN IN AUDIENCE – "You suck, McBain."

(McBain fires a machine gun into the audience.)

McBAIN – "Now, my Woody Allen impression... 'I'm a neurotic

nerd who likes to sleep with little girls'..."

MAN IN AUDIENCE – "Hey, that really sucked."

(McBain throws a grenade into the audience.)

Lisa's Wedding (2F15) 19 March 1995

When Lisa attends the Springfield Renaissance Faire a fortune-teller's cards tell of her future wedding to British subject Hugh Parkfield, who she meets at college. Hugh loves Lisa, but finds her family a sore trial, and on her wedding day tells her that after they are married they will never again see her family.

Guest Stars: Mandy Patinkin.

Blackboard: I will not strut around like I own the place.

Couch: The Simpsons are ejected from the couch and get their heads stuck in the ceiling.

What's been cut?: SKY: Some bad language, a reference to Fox turning into a 'hardcore sex channel' and a reference to a 'pornographic magazine warehouse'.

Two Dozen and One Greyhounds (2F18) 9 April 1995

Santa's Little Helper's aptitude for romance gets him a mate and the Simpsons 25 spanking new puppies. When they try to get the puppies adopted Monty Burns wants all of them, going so far as to steal them when he is turned down. Bart and Lisa set out to discover what he wants them for.

Blackboard: The Good Humor man can only be pushed so far.

Couch: The Simpsons have to chase the couch as it and the wall back away from them.

What's been cut?: SKY:

a) As Chief Wiggum and his wife watch TV:

TV ANNOUNCER – "Resist the temptation to read or talk to loved ones. Do not attempt sexual relations, as years of TV radiation have left your genitals withered and useless."

CHIEF WIGGUM – (checking under the covers) "Well I'll be damned."

b) When Santa's Little Helper shows no interest in playing fetch with Bart:

BART – "Aw. Me and Santa's Little Helper used to be a team, but he never wants to play any more since his bitch moved in."

MARGE – "Bart, don't ever say that word again!"

BART – "Well that's what she is. I looked it up."

MARGE – "Well, I'm going to write the dictionary people and have that checked. Feels like a mistake to me."

The PTA Disbands (2F19) 16 April 1995

Bart successfully manipulates the teachers and Principal Skinner into a confrontation, which guarantees a strike, and time off school for Bart. Faced with Lisa's withdrawal symptoms Marge organises the PTA to replace the teachers. Bart's new teacher is Marge – and now he has to try and get the teachers back to school or suffer at the hands of his classmates.

Blackboard: I do not have power of attorney over first graders.

Couch: Each of the Simpsons runs to the couch from a different direction in an M.C. Escher version of their house.

Phone Call For: When Moe takes over as the substitute teacher for Mrs. Krabappel's class during the strike the following dialogue takes place:

MOE – "OK, when I call your name, uh, you say 'present' or 'here'. Er, no, say 'present'. Ahem, Anita Bath?"

(The students in the classroom laugh.)

MOE – "All right, settle down. Anita Bath here?"

(More laughter.)

MOE – "All right, fine, fine. Maya Buttreeks!"

(Still more laughter)

MOE – "Hey, what are you laughing at? What? Oh, oh, I get it, I get it. It's my big ears, isn't it, kids? Isn't it? Well, children, I can't help that!"

(Runs crying from the classroom)

What's been cut?: SKY: Some violence from the 'historical re-enactment' and the expression 'half-assed'.

'Round Springfield (2F32) 30 April 1995

When Bart is rushed to hospital after swallowing a free metal Krusty-O, Lisa discovers that his fellow patient is 'Bleeding Gums' Murphy. 'Bleeding Gums' dies and Lisa discovers at his funeral that no one in town knew him, or his music. Bart receives $100,000 compensation for his cereal-related brush with death, but has only $500 dollars left after lawyers fees – and 'Bleeding Gums' only record costs just that amount.

Guest Stars: Guest stars Steve Allen and Ron Taylor.

Blackboard: Nerve gas is not a toy.

Couch: The sizes of the family are reversed as a giant Maggie, down to a tiny Homer, sit on the couch.

What's been cut?: SKY: More bad language.

The Springfield Connection (2F21) 7 May 1995

After making a citizen's arrest Marge is inspired to join the Springfield PD. She takes a serious view of her duties and ends up throwing Homer in jail. Later Homer discovers that a counterfeit jeans ring is being run out of his garage, but when Marge closes the operation down she discovers that Chief Wiggum and Co. have kept the jeans for themselves and disillusioned she resigns.

Blackboard: I will not mock Mrs. Dumbface.

Couch: A James Bond style opening, with Homer seen walking in front of the couch framed by a gun barrel. Homer draws his own gun and fires at the camera.

Lemon of Troy (2F22) 14 May 1995

Bart directs a clandestine operation in enemy territory when he and a group of Springfield children infiltrate Shelbyville to take back the town's beloved lemon tree. Homer and a party of adults, who drive into Shelbyville in Ned Flanders' RV, rescue them and return the historic tree.

Blackboard: The First Amendment does not cover burping.

Couch: In the style of an early black & white cartoon, The Simpsons wave their hands and do a bow legged bow while wearing Disney style white gloves.

Who Shot Mr. Burns? – Part One (2F16) 21 May 1995

Oil is found! Under Springfield Elementary! The school's plans for spending the money garnered from this disappear when Monty Burns finds a way of stealing it. This leads Springfield's own megalomaniac to try and control all the energy sources in the town – including the sun! Everyone has a grudge against Burns, including Homer who is driven into a state of dementia by the fact that Burns can't remember his name. When Burns is shot the suspects start to line up…

Guest Stars: Tito Puente.

Blackboard: This is not a clue…or is it?

Couch: The Simpsons run past the same TV and couch again and again, in a Hanna-Barbera cheap animation style, except for Maggie who sits there grinning.

What's been cut?: SKY: Bad language.

Season Seven (1995-1996)

Who Shot Mr. Burns? – Part Two (2F20) 17 September 1995

When Chief Wiggum finds a gun covered with his fingerprints in his car, Homer becomes suspect number one for the shooting of Montgomery Burns. Before he can be jailed Homer escapes, and the race is on to see who can reach Burns' hospital room first.

Guest Stars: Tito Puente.

Blackboard: I will not complain about the solution when I hear it.

Couch: The couch moves aside and the Simpsons line up before a police line-up height chart, while the *Dragnet* theme plays.

What's been cut?: SKY cut Snake using a flick-knife when cornered by Marge and the following exchange during Chief Wiggum's pep talk to police recruits:

RECRUIT – "Forget about the badge! When do we get the freakin' guns?!"

WIGGUM – "Hey, I told you, you don't get your gun until you tell me your name."

RECRUIT – "I've had it up to here with your 'rules'!" (walks off).

Radioactive Man (2F17) 24 September 1995

Bart and Milhouse both audition for the role of 'Fallout Boy' in the new *Radioactive Man* movie, which is being shot in Springfield. When Milhouse narrowly beats out Bart friendships are imperilled. Springfield traders and town officials begin to take the *Radioactive Man* film crew for all they can get. Then the pressure becomes too much for Milhouse...

Guest Stars: Mickey Rooney.

Blackboard: *Bewitched* does not promote Satanism.

Couch: The couch 'faxes' a life-size picture of the Simpsons from the cushions, which is ripped off and falls to the ground.

What's been cut?: SKY: Bad language...

Home Sweet Home-Diddily-Dum-Doodily (3F01) 1 October 1995

When a series of accidents makes it seem that Homer and Marge are unfit parents, Bart, Lisa and Maggie are placed in the care of Ned Flanders and family. Homer and Marge have to pass a class in child rearing to get the kids back. Just as they do, Ned finds that the kids have not been baptised and plans to baptise them – into the Flanders family.

Guest Stars: Joan Kenley.

Blackboard: No one wants to hear from my armpits.

Couch: The Simpsons, including SLH, Snowball II, and Grandpa, appear in eight squares in the style of the Brady Bunch with the couch in the middle. Everyone but Grandpa runs to the couch – he's asleep in his square!

What's been cut?: SKY: Bad language.

Bart Sells His Soul (3F02) 8 October 1995

To prove that the soul does not exist Bart sells his to Milhouse for five dollars. Soon he finds the pets behave strangely towards him and he doesn't find Itchy and Scratchy funny anymore, and suspects he has lost his soul. Trouble is, now Milhouse wants $50 for it. Meanwhile, in order to make the fullest utilisation of his army surplus deep fat fryer, Moe turns the Tavern into Uncle Moe's Family Feedbag. This episode contains the sublime moment where Bart substitutes the sheet music for Iron Butterfly's *In-A-Gadda-Da-Vida* for the church's hymn sheet.

Blackboard: I am not a lean mean spitting machine.

Couch: The Simpsons are wearing fezzes and driving around in minicars like shriners (or Akbar in *Life is Hell*). They stop facing the TV and honk their horns.

What's been cut?: SKY: A few frames from *Skinless In Seattle* the episode's Itchy & Scratchy cartoon, showing Itchy being optically impaled by the Seattle Space Needle and fluid spurting from the wound.

Lisa the Vegetarian (3F03) 15 October 1995

While visiting a local petting zoo the scales fall from Lisa's eyes and she becomes a vegetarian, unfortunately on the eve of Homer's grand barbecue. Father and daughter fall out over her hijacking of the suckling pig and Lisa goes missing in the aftermath of the argument.

Guest Stars: Paul and Linda McCartney.

Blackboard: The boys room is not a water park.

Couch: Monochrome Simpsons run to the couch, and are then spray-painted in colour.

What's been cut?: SKY: Linda McCartney plugging her own brand of vegetarian foods. Look for this one to disappear from the BBC too – remember *Boss Cat*?

Treehouse of Horror VI (3F04) 29 October 1995

The annual 'most likely to upset my kids' episode features two science fiction stories and one horror:

Attack of the 50 ft Eyesores

A strange storm brings gigantic statues of advertising characters to life in a parody of 50's monster movies.

Nightmare On Evergreen Terrace

Groundskeeper Willy is reincarnated as a Freddy Kruger wannabe after he is burned alive at a PTA meeting. He pursues his revenge in the dreams of Springfield's children.

Homer^3

In a parody of the *Little Girl Lost* episode of *The Twilight Zone* Homer discovers a 3D dimension when hiding from Patty and Selma. The dimension collapses in on itself propelling Homer into our world.

Guest Stars: Paul Anka.

Couch: The Simpsons drop from above, hung from their necks by nooses; Maggie still manages to suck her pacifier.

What's been cut?: It's Treehouse time again, time for SKY to get out the censor's knife...

a) The opening couch gag, which features the family dropping from the ceiling one at a time, heads in nooses and eyes open has gone.

b) In *Attack of the 50 ft Eyesores* Lard Lad boots a barking dog like a football and rakes his donut over the roofs of the houses.

c) During the sequence in which Willie burns to death, a segment contrasting his struggle with the furnace with the school budget for safety equipment being cut has gone.

d) Willie in the PTA meeting as his flesh burns from his bones has gone. Perhaps we should be glad...

King-Size Homer (3F05) 5 November 1995

Homer discovers that if he has a disability he can work from home. And obesity counts as a disability... Pretty soon Homer has reached his target weight of 300 pounds, and can work at home, where he deputes a novelty bobbing head bird to duplicate his keyboard work while he visits the movies. The bird fails, leading to the reactor core approaching meltdown. Homer saves the plant by inadvertently blocking a leak with his body and Monty Burns rewards him by paying for his liposuction.

Guest Stars: Joan Kenley.

Blackboard: Indian burns are not our cultural heritage.

Couch: The Simpsons rush in as wind-up dolls and robotically make their way to the couch.

What's been cut?: SKY: Minor bad language.

Mother Simpson (3F06) 19 November 1995

When Homer fakes his own death to avoid a litter collecting detail, he discovers that the tombstone his father has told him is his mother's, isn't. His mother comes to say her goodbyes to her (ostensibly) dead son, and Homer and family discover that she is on the run from the FBI for the events of 25 years previously. And Monty Burns has identified the fugitive...

Guest Stars: Glenn Close and Harry Morgan.

Couch: The Simpsons are placed on the couch by a pinsetter from ten-pin bowling, after Snowball II is scared off by the pin-clearing bar.

What's been cut?: SKY: When Homer finds that the tombstone he thought was his mom's is Walt Whitman's grave, quite a bit has been cut...

HOMER – "Aargh! Damn you, Walt Whitman! (repeatedly kicks grave) I! Hate! You! Walt! Freaking! Whitman! 'Leaves of Grass', my ass!"

…and when Abe meets his wife again after twenty-seven years, after stating she was a rotten wife and that he doesn't forgive her, he goes on to say:

ABE – "Can we have sex? Please?"

GRANDMA – "Oh, Abe."

ABE – "Well, I tried! What's for supper?"

Sideshow Bob's Last Gleaming (3F08) 26 November 1995

Sideshow Bob has become obsessed by the negative impact of TV on society and slips away from a work detail on an Air Force base and steals an atomic bomb. He threatens to detonate it unless the town of Springfield gives up television. But Krusty the Clown doesn't intend to give up stardom that easily.

Guest Stars: R. Lee Ermey and Kelsey Grammer.

Blackboard: Wedgies are unhealthy for children and other living things.

Couch: The Simpsons are sea-monkeys and swim to a couch made of clamshells. They stare at a treasure chest instead of the TV.

What's been cut?: SKY cut the following:

a) An odd piece of dialogue censorship:

BOB – (picking up rubbish) "There. That's the last condom wrapper."

b) When Bob laments that "TV's bottomless chum-bucket has claimed Vanessa Redgrave!" the following dialogue is missing:

REDGRAVE – "Now I'm gonna haul ass to Lollapalooza! Yeehaa!"

(TV Audience laughs) BOB – "Farewell, dear 'Nessa…"

(The 20th Century Fox theme plays.)

c) In the underground bunker when Hapablap laments the amount of porn found on the base a shot of several porn magazines has been cut.

d) In the blimp, Bart and Lisa trying to stall Sideshow Bob nearly all the dialogue between Bart and Bob is cut so that Bob's knife wielding isn't seen:

BOB – "Let's not embarrass us both with that hoary old 'stall the villain with flattery' scheme."

BART – "I should have known you were too smart to fall for that."

BOB – (wielding knife) "Really? What type of smart? Book smart? Because there are a lot of people who are book smart but it takes a special type of genius to – "

e) This complete scene is cut after Homer starts the chase for Sideshow Bob:

(Bob has Bart in the Wright Brothers plane and is holding the knife to him.)

BOB – "Aah, for the days when aviation was a gentleman's pursuit

– back before every Joe Sweatsock could wedge himself behind a lunch tray and jet off to Raleigh-Durham."

BART – (spitting) "Are you getting lots of bugs in your mouth too?"

BOB – (pause) "Yeah." (spits)

There's also censorship of minor swearing.

The Simpsons 138th Episode Spectacular! (3F31) 3 December 1995

Troy McClure hosts an half- hour show looking back at The Simpsons' past eight-year history, including out-takes from previous shows. There is new material from *Krusty Gets Kancelled* (9F19) *$pringfield* (1F08) *Mother Simpson* (3F06) *Treehouse of Horror IV* (1F04) *Homer and Apu* (1F10) *Burns' Heir* (1F16) and the alternate ending to *Who Shot Mr. Burns? Part Two* (2F20) as well as a nice series of clips from the *Tracey Ullman Show* shorts.

Blackboard: I will only do this once a year.

Couch: The Simpsons are swallowed by the couch as it transforms into a monster. *Also:* The Simpsons form a chorus line, and are joined by the Rockettes, circus animals, jugglers, trapeze artists, magicians, fire breathers and Santa's Little Helper (amongst others) for a musical spectacular. *And:* A tiny Simpsons family rushes in and starts to climb the giant couch; Maggie has to be pulled up. *In addition:* The Simpsons rush in and sit, just before the room is filled with what seems like most of Springfield. *And...* aw, check them out yourselves – the episode uses the couch gags from 8F18, 9F02, 9F10, 9F09, 8F09, 1F02, 2F31, 2F09, 2F06, 1F17, 2F11, and 2F08.

What's been cut?: There's some irony in that these cuts are in out-takes from previous shows. Thanks, SKY...

1) At the beginning of the out-take from 9F19 – Krusty Gets Cancelled:

KRUSTY – "...watch my show, I will send you this book featuring me in a variety of sexually explicit positions... (some men drag him off) What? Hey! It's not really me: I used a stunt butt!"

2) The out-take from 1F16 – *Burns' Heir*, as the robotic Richard Simmons starts to get out of control.

SMITHERS – "His ass is going to blow!!"

Marge Be Not Proud (3F07) 17 December 1995

Lusting after the new video game *Bonestorm*, Bart is apprehended for shoplifting and warned to never return to the store. He manages to keep it a secret from Homer and Marge, but Marge's destination for the family Christmas photo is the same store...

Guest Stars: Lawrence Tierney.

Blackboard: I will stop talking about the twelve inch pianist.

Couch: Homer pulls a drain plug from the floor, and The Simpsons and the contents of the room are sucked into the drain.

Team Homer (3F10) 7 January 1996

A drugged Monty Burns provides an astonished Homer with the registration fee Homer needs to start his bowling team the 'Pin Pals'. When Burns comes to he decides to join the team, with predictably disastrous results. Meanwhile, Bart's 'Down with Homework' T-shirt incites a riot at school, resulting in Principal Skinner issuing school uniforms.

Blackboard: I am not certified to remove asbestos.

Couch: The Simpsons sit, as the camera moves to the inside of a mouse hole where a family of mice Simpsons sit on an identical couch.

What's been cut?: SKY cut the scene following the team being asked for the registration fee:

MARGE – "No, I will not pay you $500 for sex!"

HOMER – "Aw, come on, Marge. You're getting something in return, and I'm getting a bowling team. it's win-win!"

MARGE – "It's sick! And I don't have that kind of money to spend on sex."

Two Bad Neighbors (3F09) 14 January 1996

When George and Barbara Bush move in across the road from the Simpsons Homer is annoyed by the amount of attention given to them. After playing Mr Wilson to Bart's Dennis the Menace (US variety) the former President gives Bart a spanking, leading to a war developing between Homer and George.

Couch: A big game hunter sits on the couch. There is a Homer-skin rug on the floor and the rest of the family form trophies on the wall.

Scenes from the Class Struggle in Springfield (3F11) 4 February 1996

Marge's purchase of a Chanel suit for $90 and a chance encounter with an old classmate yields an invitation to the Springfield Country Club. Marge is a success, and the family are invited back. Homer plays golf with Monty Burns, and uses his discovery that Smithers cheats for his boss to blackmail a membership of the club for Marge. But Marge's Chanel suit is wearing out and no more bargains are available…

Guest Stars: Tom Kite.

Couch: The Simpsons sit and are bathed in black light, until Homer turns on the lamp.

Bart the Fink (3F12) 11 February 1996

When Bart can't get Krusty's autograph he gives him a cheque for

25 cents, knowing Krusty has to endorse it. When it comes back to Bart it is stamped as endorsed in the Cayman Islands. The bank teller Bart complains to informs the IRS and Krusty is exposed as a tax cheat.

A depressed Krusty the Clown pilots his plane into the side of a mountain. But wait – who's this bearded, but blue haired, sailor?

Guest Stars: Bob Newhart.

Couch: The couch 'faxes' a life-size picture of the Simpsons from the cushions, which is ripped off and falls to the ground.

What's been cut?: SKY censored the following:

a) From the scene with the Cayman Islands guy:

"Oh, crap. I shouldn't have said he was a customer... Oh, crap. I shouldn't have said it was a secret... Oh, crap! I certainly shouldn't have said it was illegal. (sighs) It's too hot today."

b) After Krusty (as Rory B. Bellows) forgets that his boat is still moored when he tries to sail away:

KRUSTY – "You know, you kids coulda said something instead of letting me make an ass of myself."

c) When Krusty throws the Global Positioning System overboard:

KRUSTY – "Tell me where you are now, you bastard."

Lisa the Iconoclast (3F13) 18 February 1996

It's Springfield's bicentennial, and Homer is appointed town cryer for the celebrations. But Lisa discovers that Jebediah Springfield, the town founder, isn't a hero but a silver-tongued (literally!) pirate who (amongst other things) tried to kill George Washington, and forces an exhumation of Jebediah to prove her case...

Guest Stars: Donald Sutherland.

Couch: The Simpsons, including SLH, Snowball II, and Grandpa, appear in eight squares in the style of the Brady Bunch with the couch in the middle. Everyone but Grandpa runs to the couch – he's asleep in his square!

Homer the Smithers (3F14) 25 February 1996

Monty Burns insists that Smithers takes a much-needed vacation. To make sure he's not replaced he hires Homer as his temporary replacement. Unfortunately Homer hits Burns and Burns, in fear of his life, learns how to cope for himself. When Smithers returns Burns fires him, as he no longer needs him. Happily Smithers and Homer fight, defenestrating Burns, who, confined to bed, needs Smithers to care for him again.

Couch: The Simpsons are wearing fezzes and driving around in minicars like shriners (or Akbar in *Life is Hell*.)

Phone Call For: Monty Burns is mistaken for a prank caller when he calls for Smithers (see below) showing that Moe will *never* get the hang of the prank call business.

What's been cut?: When Moe mistakes Monty Burns' request for 'a Mr. Smithers, first name Waylon' for a crank call the following dialogue was cut by SKY from 'so you can watch me' onwards:

MOE – "When I catch you, I'm gonna pull out your eyes, and shove 'em down your pants so you can watch me kick the crap outta you, okay? Then I'm gonna use your tongue to paint my boat!"

The Day the Violence Died (3F16) 17 March 1996

Bart meets Chester J Lampwick, who claims he invented Itchy and Scratchy who were stolen from him by Roger Meyers Sr. Bart, with the help of Lionel Hutz mounts a claim on Roger Meyers Jr's studio and bankrupts it, meaning no more Itchy & Scratchy. As Bart and Lisa seek a way to restore Itchy & Scratchy to the televisions of the nation, Lester and Eliza, two children with a scary resemblance to the two Simpson children save Itchy & Scratchy.

Couch: Monochrome Simpsons run to the couch, and are then spray-painted in colour.

Guest Stars: Alex Rocco, Jack Sheldon, Suzanne Somers and Kirk Douglas as Chester J. Lampwick, the original Itchy creator.

What's been cut?: SKY cut the following:

a) In the *Remembrance of Things Slashed* Itchy & Scratchy cartoon, a section of Itchy stabbing the ghost of Scratchy has been pasted over with a repeated shot from earlier in the cartoon. You can freeze frame a tape of the segment and see the few frames of demented mouse plus knife at each end of the section.

b) While Bart and Milhouse watch Itchy's debut in *Manhattan Madness* the following has been cut:

MILHOUSE – "Come on, Itchy! Kill that guy! (reading the on-screen cue card aloud) 'A Chance for more mischief'."

Enter a cartoon Teddy Roosevelt.

BART – (over the cartoon) "Look at that fat oaf!" (laughs)

MILHOUSE – (over the cartoon) "It's Teddy Roosevelt."

(The next cue card says 'Ah, Manhattan Town. An agreeable sight for an Old Knickerbocker such as myself'. Itchy grabs an axe and chops Roosevelt's head off. Covered in blood he winks at the camera.)

A Fish Called Selma (3F15) 24 March 1996

When Troy McClure swaps a date with Selma in exchange for her turning a blind eye to his poor vision test for his drivers license his film career is given a boost when he is seen dating a woman. To stay in the public eye, Troy ends up marrying Selma for the publicity.

Guest Stars: Jeff Goldblum.

Couch: The Simpsons rush in as wind-up dolls and robotically make their way to the couch.

Bart on the Road (3F17) 31 March 1996

When Principal Skinner closes school a day early the output of Bart's day with Patty and Selma is a fake drivers ID. Bart runs into Nelson, Martin and Milhouse and armed with money and fake ID rent a car and head for Knoxville Tennessee for the World's Fair. Unfortunately it ended fourteen years earlier, and their car is destroyed. Lisa, who has spent Spring Break with Homer at the power plant persuades Homer to order equipment for the plant and route it via Knoxville, where the boys stow away in the crate.

Couch: The Simpsons are placed on the couch by a pinsetter from ten-pin bowling, after Snowball II is scared off by the pin-clearing bar.

Phone Call For: Homer perpetrates this one:

HOMER – "Hello, I'd like to speak with a Mr. Snotball, first name Ura."

MOE – "Ura Snotball?"

HOMER – "What? How dare you? If I find out who this is, I'll staple a flag to your butt and mail you to Iran." (hangs up)

22 Short Films About Springfield (3F18) 14 April 1996

One of the best episodes ever, as Bart and Milhouse wonder if anything of interest ever happens in Springfield, and we are taken through a series of vignettes about the town and its inhabitants. The episode title is taken from *Thirty-Two Short Films About Glenn Gould* (but obviously they had to economise) and includes two *Pulp Fiction* parodies as Chief Wiggum and Lou discuss the relative merits of Krustyburger and McDonalds and later when Milhouse instigates Herman's hostage taking spree.

Couch: The Simpsons are sea-monkeys who swim to a couch made of clamshells, and stare at a treasure chest instead of the TV.

Raging Abe Simpson and His Grumbling Grandson in 'The Curse of the Flying Hellfish' (3F19) 28 April 1996

After being embarrassed by his stories Bart learns that Grandpa and Mr. Burns served together in World War II and have a share in treasure distributed through a tontine – an arrangement where the last surviving member gets the loot. Now Abe and Monty are the last survivors, but Monty Burns wants to speed the process up a little.

Couch: Homer pulls a drain plug from the floor, and The Simpsons and the contents of the room are sucked into the drain.

Much Apu About Nothing (3F20) 5 May 1996

To distract the citizens of Springfield from his tax hike Mayor Quimby blames high taxes on immigrants and gives birth to Proposition 24 – a law calling for the deportation of all immigrants from Springfield. Homer is a Proposition 24 enthusiast – until he discovers Apu is an illegal immigrant. Lisa finds that Apu qualifies for an amnesty and can become an American citizen – if he can pass the citizenship test.

Guest Stars: Joe Mantegna.

Couch: A big game hunter sits on the couch. There is a Homer-skin rug on the floor and the rest of the family form trophies on the wall.

What's been cut?: SKY cut a car crash after Diana's death but later restored it.

Homerpalooza (3F21) 19 May 1996

Discovering his kids think of him as terminally uncool Homer buys tickets to the Hullabalooza touring rock festival and ends up as part of it, in the travelling freak show catching cannon balls with his belly. As the tour progresses his stomach starts complaining. Warned to stop by a veterinarian, his next gig is in front of his hometown of Springfield.

Guest Stars: Cypress Hill, Peter Frampton, The Smashing Pumpkins and Sonic Youth.

Couch: The Simpsons sit and are bathed in black light, until Homer turns on the lamp.

What's been cut?: When Peter Frampton's inflatable pig makes a break for freedom the following deathless dialogue has been cut by SKY:

TECH – "Aw, man. There goes Peter Frampton's big finale. He's gonna be pissed off."

FRAMPTON – "You're damn right I'm going to be pissed off – I bought that pig at Pink Floyd's yard sale!"

Summer of 4 Ft. 2 (3F22) 19 May 1996

Finding that she is one of the least popular girls in school when no one signs her yearbook, Lisa determines to change. Homer is looking after the Flanders beach cottage for the summer, and Lisa dresses as a Gen X slacker and makes friends with the local cool kids. But Bart, annoyed by her social success, shows her friends her yearbook...

Guest Stars: Christina Ricci.

Couch: The couch 'faxes' a life-size picture of the Simpsons from the cushions, which is ripped off and falls to the ground.

What's been cut?: SKY cut the following:

a) As Homer attempts to buy illegal fireworks the following section of the scene in the L'il Valu Mart has been cut:

Homer wanders over to the counter, whistling and trying to act natural.

HOMER – "Hi... Umm... Let me have some of those porno magazines... Large box of condoms... A bottle of ol' Harper... A couple of those panty shields (quickly) and some illegal fireworks (normal speech) and one of those disposable enemas. Er, make it two."

b) Back at the holiday home:

(Marge looks through the items Homer has purchased – the porno magazine has 'America's largest Breakfast' on the cover.)

MARGE – "I don't know what you have planned tonight, but count me out... (Homer takes the firework) Didn't you buy any meat?"

Season Eight (1996-1997)

Treehouse of Horror VII (4F02) 27 October 1996

One of the less nauseating Halloween episodes for those of you with kids:

The Thing and I

Bart discovers that he has an 'evil twin' brother locked away in the Simpsons' attic. Based on any 'evil-twin-in-the-attic' book or movie you like.

The Genesis Tub

Lisa creates a culture from her tooth dissolved in soda, which develops into a microverse, where Lisa is worshipped as God and Bart reviled as the Devil. Inspired by the *Twilight Zone* episode *The Little People.*

Citizen Kang

Our friendly neighbourhood aliens Kang and Kodos kidnap and impersonate Bob Dole and Bill Clinton in the run-up to the election, and Homer must expose their evil plot for world domination.

Couch: The Grim Reaper sits on the couch. The Simpsons run up to the couch and fall over dead. The Reaper puts his feet up on Homer.

You Only Move Twice (3F23) 3 November 1996

When Waylon Smithers turns it down, as the next longest serving power plant employee Homer is offered a job by Globex. The Simpsons move to Cypress Creek, which at first seems ideal. But Homer's touchy-feely boss Hank Scorpio is a super villain who is out to rule the world, and Cypress Creek is not as ideal as it first seems.

Guest Stars: Albert Brooks.

Blackboard: I did not learn everything I need to know in kindergarten.

Couch: The Simpsons land on the couch via parachute except Homer, who lands on the floor with an unopened chute.

The Homer They Fall (4F03) 10 November 1996

When he discovers that Homer can absorb massive blows to the head Moe turns him into a successful boxer. Marge is worried that won't save Homer in the upcoming match with Dreaderick Tatum, the heavyweight champion.

Guest Stars: Michael Buffer and Paul Winfield.

Blackboard: I am not my long-lost twin.

Couch: The Simpsons are dressed as cowfolk and the living room a western plain. They ride the couch into the sunset.

What's been cut?: SKY cuts:

a) The title sequence has been cut:

Blackboard: I am not my long lost twin.

Couch Gag: The couch is outside in a western desert. Everyone is in cowboy gear as they sit on it and gallop away.

Why these have been cut no-one knows...

b) A piece of dialogue from Moe...

MOE – "Okey-doke. Future's down the crapper. Gotcha."

Burns, Baby Burns (4F05) 17 November 1996

When Month Burns discovers his long lost 60-year-old illegitimate son Larry, he soon tires of his oafish behaviour, and rejects him. Homer helps Larry to stage a fake kidnapping to change Burns' mind.

Guest Stars: Rodney Dangerfield.

Couch: The Simpsons float in as soap bubbles, which float onto the couch and pop.

What's been cut?: SKY, bad language.

Bart After Dark (4F06) 24 November 1996

While Lisa and Marge have gone to help clear up after an oil spill, Bart causes damage to an old spooky house. Homer, trying to do what Marge would have done, forces Bart to work for the homeowner, unaware that she runs Maison Derriere, a burlesque house. Bart quickly ends up running the door of the house, but on Marge's return 'concerned citizens' want the place closed down. Contains one of the best songs in the show 'The Spring in Springfield'.

Couch: A parody of the cover of The Beatles' Sgt. Pepper's Lonely Hearts Club Band featuring (among others) the original Tracey Ullman Simpsons, the head of Jebediah Springfield, Grandpa's revitalising tonic, and 'The Simpsons' spelled out in donuts.

What's been cut?: Some 'erotic' high kicking from the ladies of Maison Derriere.

A Milhouse Divided (4F04) 1 December 1996

At the latest in a long line of disastrous Simpsons parties, Kirk and Luann Van Houten (Milhouse's parents) announce their divorce. Homer, realising he has taken his marriage for granted, becomes increasingly certain that the same is going to happen to him and Marge.

Couch: The Simpsons enter with Bart behaving like a faulty TV picture. He starts off green; As Homer changes TV channels Bart turns red. Homer slaps Bart on the head, changing him to normal.

What's been cut?: The following scene was cut by SKY:

(Luanne Van Houten sings to herself as she packs a box full of her ex's clothes.)

MARGE – "I must say, Luanne, you're really handling this splendidly."

(Luanne pours lighter fluid over the box and sets it alight.)

LUANNE – "From now on, forget everything you thought you knew about Luanne Van Houten."

MARGE – "Actually, Luanne, I don't really know anything about you – "

LUANNE – "Forget it! She's gone. Prest-o change-o! Kaboom! Sweet Fanny Adams! Bye-bye!"

Lisa's Date with Density (4F01) 15 December 1996

Homer finds a phone autodialler and uses it for a telemarketing fraud, while Lisa develops a crush on bully Nelson Muntz and tries to change him, with predictable results.

Couch: Simpsons and couch are upside-down and the Simpsons fall off the couch and onto the 'ceiling'.

Hurricane Neddy (4F07) 29 December 1996

A hurricane hits Springfield and only Ned Flanders house is destroyed. He and his family move into the church's basement where he discovers the Leftorium has been looted. When he lashes out in anger at the Springfieldians who have helped (ineptly) to rebuild his house he fears a breakdown and commits himself to a mental institution, where we learn more about Ned's parents and history.

Couch: Homer puts a coin in a Vend-A-Couch machine on the wall, and nothing happens. He then bangs the wall and the couch falls on him.

What's been cut?: SKY cut the scene where Homer is attempting to annoy Ned Flanders at the mental hospital:

NED – "Oh, well, I'll just have to try harder. Heh heh. Thanks for dropping by."

(partition slides up)

DR FOSTER – "Ah, he's still repressing. (into microphone) Maximum hostility factor."

(partition slides down)

HOMER – "I engaged in intercourse with your spouse or significant other. (to the doctors) Now that's psychiatry! Eh? Eh?"

El Viaje Misterioso de Nuestro Homer (aka The Mysterious Voyage of Homer) (3F24) 5 January1997

When Homer tastes Chief Wiggum's chilli, made with Guatemalan peppers he goes on an hallucinatory spiritual journey, and meets a mystical coyote who makes him question whether or not Marge is his soulmate.

Guest Stars: Johnny Cash.

Couch: The Simpsons land on the couch via parachute except Homer, who lands on the floor with an unopened chute.

What's been cut?: Bizarrely SKY chose to cut a scene with Homer drinking and then spitting out a candle (don't ask – watch the episode…):

RALPH: "Wait, mister, you're drinking a candle. You don't want to get wax in your mouth, do you?"

HOMER: (slyly) "Maybe I do, son. Maybe I do."

(Homer chugs the candle, and spits out a stream of wax, which solidifies on the spot.)

HOMER: "Outstanding!"

Why, we'll never know…

The Springfield Files (3G01) 12 January 1997

Returning drunk from Moe's, Homer sees an alien creature in Springfield woods. No one will believe him – even FBI agents Fox Mulder and Dana Scully (from The X-Files) question his credibility. Bart and Homer stalk the creature and videotape it, setting the scene for hundreds of Springfieldians to gather on the date of the next likely appearance.

Guest Stars: Gillian Anderson, David Duchovny and Leonard Nimoy.

Blackboard: The truth is not out there.

Couch: The Simpsons fly onto the couch using jet-packs; Maggie flies in last and lands on Marge's lap.

The Twisted World of Marge Simpson (4F08) 19 January 1997

When Marge is voted out of the Springfield Investorettes for being too cautious she buys a pretzel franchise. Unfortunately it fails, until Homer asks Fat Tony, Springfield's local mobster for help. Marge is overjoyed until Fat Tony wants his share of the proceedings. Meanwhile the Investorettes, who have started a falafel franchise, have done a deal with the Yakuza...

Guest Stars: Jack Lemmon and Joe Mantegna.

Blackboard: I am not licensed to do anything.

Couch: The Simpsons substitute for the mole in a giant game of Whack-A-Mole; their heads all pop out of holes and Homer ends up getting whacked.

What's been cut?: SKY: When Marge's rivals introduce the Yakuza to her the following dialogue is cut from 'the Poison Fists'...

MAUDE – "perhaps you've heard of the Yakuza – the Poison Fists of the Pacific Rim. The Japanese mafia!"

AGNES – "They'll kill ya five times before you hit the ground!"

Mountain of Madness (4F10) 2 February 1997

Promoting team work amongst the power plant's employees Monty Burns makes them go on a survival retreat up in the mountains. The goal: to find a cabin hidden on the snowy mountainside. Burns ends up teamed with Homer and at first things go well, due to the use of a hidden snowmobile. The pair dig in at the cabin, which is promptly buried by an avalanche, as all the other teams converge on a ranger station that they mistake for the cabin. Meanwhile Homer and Burns are buried alive and going insane from the cold...

Couch: Grandpa is sleeping on the couch which is folded out to make a couch bed. The Simpsons enter and convert it to a sofa (with Grandpa in it) and sit on it.

Simpsoncalifragilisticexpiala(Annoyed Grunt)cious (3G03) 7 February 1997

When Marge's luxurious tresses start to fall out due to overwork and stress the Simpson family get a nanny. With an umbrella. And the power of flight. Called Shary Bobbins.

Blackboard: I will not hide the teacher's Prozac.

Couch: The couch remains empty while The Simpsons wait outside as Homer struggles to unlock the front door.

The Itchy & Scratchy & Poochie Show (4F12) 9 February 1997

This is the 167th episode, the episode where *The Simpsons* surpassed *The Flintstones* as television's longest-running, animated prime-time series. As the ratings of *The Itchy and Scratchy Show* plummet the producers decide to add Poochie, a 'hip' dog. And Homer provides Poochie's voice...

Guest Stars: Alex Rocco.

Couch: A parody of the cover of The Beatles' Sgt. Pepper's Lonely

Hearts Club Band featuring (among others) the original Tracey Ullman Simpsons, the head of Jebediah Springfield, Grandpa's revitalising tonic, and 'The Simpsons' spelled out in donuts.

What's been cut?: Given that this is kind of a special episode, SKY went to town on it:

a) The couch gag has been modified. Originally the same as 4F06, *Bart After Dark*, a parody of the Sgt Pepper album sleeve the visuals have been replaced with 8F24 – the Simpsons find the Flintstones on the couch. You can see the point, but the sound track from the first opening has been left.

b) At the beginning of the show an entire Itchy & Scratchy episode *Why Do Fools Fall In Lava?* has been cut:

Tourist Scratchy visits a volcano with a bungee jump, operated by Itchy. After he pays for the jump, Itchy slashes him open with a knife, ties his intestines to the railing, and pushes him over the edge. Luckily, his fall is broken by his entrails, suspending him a few feet over the lava. Above him Itchy inserts a funnel into Scratchy's intestine and is pouring petrol into it. Scratchy frantically tries to cover his mouth to keep any petrol from escaping, but his cheeks swell up, and as the petrol bursts from his mouth he is burned to a crisp.

c) Mild swearing by Otto and June Bellamy.

Homer's Phobia (4F11) 16 February 1997

Trying to sell a family heirloom (which turns out to be a liquor bottle) the Simpsons befriend the shop owner. Homer belatedly finds out that he is homosexual and becomes worried Bart will emulate him. Finding Bart in a wig doing the *In His Kiss* (the Shoop Shoop song) Homer decides to try and inculcate 'manliness' in him, and they depart on an ill-advised hunting trip...

Guest Stars: John Waters.

Couch: The couch is shown in an 'America Onlink' window, which slowly loads the Simpsons before an off-screen presence clicks the Exit button.

The Brother From Another Series (4F14) 23 February 1997

When Sideshow Bob is released on the recommendation of Reverend Lovejoy he reunites with his estranged bother Cecil. We learn that it was Cecil's audition for Krusty's sidekick that got Bob the part, robbing Cecil of his life's ambition. Cecil is now a Hydrological Engineer and he puts Bob in charge of the building of Springfield's Hydroelectric Dam. Bart suspects a sinister scheme and dogs Bob's footprints – but the truth is stranger than Bart can imagine... For anyone who doesn't know (Hi! Where have you been?) David Hyde Pierce plays Kelsey (Sideshow Bob) Grammer's brother in *Frasier.*

Guest Stars: Kelsey Grammer and David Hyde Pierce.

Couch: Simpsons and couch are upside-down and the Simpsons fall off the couch and onto the 'ceiling'.

My Sister, My Sitter (4F13) 2 March 1997

Lisa builds a reputation as an ace babysitter, wise beyond her years. Until the night she has to babysit her older brother Bart...

Couch: The couch is on a ship's deck, moving to and fro with the motion of the ship. The Simpsons (dressed in sou'westers) sit on it and are hit by a wave.

What's been cut?: Some bad language by SKY. After this season SKY seemed to lose heart and words like 'ass' and 'crap' have tended to be left in.

Homer vs. the Eighteenth Amendment (4F15) 16 March 1997

After a St Patrick's Day accident leaves a drunken Bart on display to all who watch TV in Springfield, an old prohibition law is bought into force. Rex Banner, an Elliot Ness-alike replaces Chief Wiggum, and Homer goes into the bootlegging business. At first he simply digs up discarded barrels of Duff from the city dump, but later he moves into full-time manufacturing.

Guest Stars: Dave Thomas and Joe Mantegna.

Couch: The Simpsons are dressed as cowfolk and the living room is a western plain. They ride the couch into the sunset.

What's been cut?: Various SKY cuts of various degrees of sense:

a) At The St. Patrick's Day parade the 'John Bull's Fish & Chip shop' explodes and everyone cheers.

b) At Moe's as the regulars watch the parade on TV Homer puts a barrel over his head and claims:

HOMER – "Look at me! I'm the Prime Minister of Ireland!"

c) When Rex Banner rejects Fat Tony's bribe the following dialogue was cut:

FAT TONY – "From now on, we'll stick to smuggling heroin."

BANNER – "See that you do."

Grade School Confidential (4F09) 6 April 1997

Bart discovers that Principal Skinner and Mrs. Krabappel are involved in an affair and he arranges to swap his permanent record for Milhouse's in return for keeping it a secret. Finding himself increasingly involved (and embarrassingly so) in their romance as a go-between, Bart exposes their love to the school, a situation that leads to their sacking...

Couch: The Simpsons float onto the couch as soap bubbles and pop.

The Canine Mutiny (4F16) 13 April 1997

Bart gets a credit card issued in Santa's Little Helper's name (Santos L Halper) and buys a purebred collie called Laddie with it. When the repo men turn up Bart gives them Santa's Little Helper instead of Laddie, and immediately regrets it. So begins a search that will end with large quantities of marijuana, beer and reggae music (and that's just the cops.)

Guest Stars: Frank Welker.

Blackboard: A fire drill does not demand a fire.

Couch: Grandpa is sleeping on the couch which is folded out to make a couch bed. The Simpsons enter and convert it to a sofa (with Grandpa in it) and sit on it.

The Old Man and the Lisa (4F17) 20 April 1997

When Monty Burns loses his vast fortune Lisa tries to instruct him in concern for the environment. Unfortunately Monty doesn't quite get the message and Lisa ends up making the unpleasant tycoon richer than ever in a more disgusting way than ever.

Guest Stars: Bret 'the Hitman' Hart.

Couch: The Simpsons substitute for the mole in a giant game of Whack-A-Mole; their heads all pop out of holes and Homer ends up getting whacked.

In Marge We Trust (4F18) 27 April 1997

Marge finds herself replacing Reverend Lovejoy as the person people turn to for help when he loses interest in helping people. She becomes a popular seer in Springfield, until she gives advice to Ned 'kiss of death' Flanders. Homer is disturbed when he finds his face on a box of dish soap from Japan.

Guest Stars: Sab Shimono, Gedde Watanabe and Frank Welker.

Couch: Homer puts a coin in a Vend-A-Couch machine on the wall, and nothing happens. He then bangs the wall and the couch falls on him.

Homer's Enemy (4F19) 4 May 1997

A new employee at the power plant, Frank Grimes, initially unimpressed with Homer's bad habits and lack of any work ethic, becomes seriously annoyed when he sees Homer's house, wife and kids and sees that Homer is more of a success than he is. His plots to expose Homer to ridicule backfire with unfortunate consequences for Grimes...

Guest Stars: Frank Welker.

Couch: The Simpsons enter with Bart behaving like a faulty TV picture. He starts off green; As Homer changes TV channels Bart turns red. Homer slaps Bart on the head, changing him to normal.

The Simpsons Spinoff Showcase (4F20) 11 May 1997

The talented Troy McClure presents three Simpsons spin-off shows:

Chief Wiggum, P.I.

Chief Wiggum takes Principal Skinner to New Orleans as his assistant in a new venture: he's going to try detective work...

The Love-Matic Grandpa

Grandpa Simpson's soul gives romantic advice to Moe from its new location: trapped inside Moe's Love Tester machine.

The Simpson Family Smile-Time Variety Hour

The Simpson family host a show eerily reminiscent of the Andy Williams Show.

Guest Stars: Tim Conway and Gailard Sartain.

The Secret War of Lisa Simpson (4F21) 18 May 1997

As punishment for a worse prank than usual, Homer and Marge register Bart in a Military Academy. Lisa insists on going too against the advice of the Commandant and is subjected to resentment and hazing. She is determined to stick it out.

Guest Stars: Willem Dafoe.

Couch: Simpsons and couch are upside-down and the Simpsons fall off the couch and onto the 'ceiling'.

Season Nine (1997-1998)

The City of New York vs. Homer Simpson (4F22) 21 September 1997

When Barney Gumble is voted designated driver for the night he manages it, but then disappears for two months with Homer's car. Homer finds his car has been abandoned in downtown Manhattan, the place he hates most in the world. When the family goes to retrieve their property, Homer finds it's worse than he'd thought.

Couch: The Simpsons enter dressed as Harlem Globetrotters to the tune of *Sweet Georgia Brown.*

The Principal and the Pauper (4F23) 28 September 1997

While attending a banquet honouring his twenty years as principal, Seymour Skinner is revealed as an impostor when the real Seymour returns from a secret POW camp in Vietnam. Skinner is really Armin

Tamzarian, a no-good street punk from Capitol City, who stole Skinner's identity when he was reported as dead. Tamzarian tries to return to his old life. It soon becomes clear that Springfield prefers Tamzarian as Skinner, including Skinner's mom.

Guest Stars: Martin Sheen.

Couch: The Simpsons rush to the couch dressed as astronauts: the couch then lifts off into space.

Lisa's Sax (3G02) 1 October 1997

Lisa's saxophone is destroyed in a struggle with Bart. Later the story of how she got her instrument during the heat wave of 1990 is told.

Guest Stars: Fyvush Finkel.

Blackboard: I no longer want my MTV.

Couch: Homer stands in front of the couch; the top half of his body then comes off (and lands on the couch) revealing Marge, then in succession Bart, Lisa, and Maggie.

What's been cut?: SKY has cut Homer's recollection of his father's words from his first day at school:

ABE – "Homer you're as dumb as a mule and twice as ugly, if a strange man in a car offers you a ride, I say take!"

Treehouse of Horror VIII (5F02) 26 October 1997

Time again for the annual episode most likely to freak out your kids. At the start of this episode a Fox censor is stabbed to death while making cuts in the episode's script, and collapses in a welter of blood. My five-year-old daughter ran screaming from the room, teaching me a valuable lesson about the Halloween episodes and small kids. While the sexual allusions in the show tend to go over their heads, the Halloween episodes can (seriously) give them nightmares, probably made worse by the fact they are rarely shown in context (i.e. *at* Halloween). I check to see which episodes SKY or the BBC are showing now before agreeing they can see *The Simpsons.*

The Homega Man

A parody of *The Omega Man* (based on Richard Matheson's *I Am Legend*). When Springfield is destroyed in a nuclear blast Homer has to battle the horribly mutated survivors.

Fly Vs. Fly

A parody of (well duh!) *The Fly*, Bart uses one of Professor Frink's discarded inventions to try to become a superhero. He becomes half-Bart half-housefly instead and mirthful mayhem ensues (sorry, I've always wanted to use that phrase).

Easy-Bake Coven

In colonial America Marge is accused of witchcraft. Hilarity ensues (sorry).

Couch: The Simpsons sit on the couch: electric chair type helmets drop onto their heads from the ceiling and they are strapped to the couch and electrocuted.

The Cartridge Family (5F01) 02 November1997

After the appearance of the Continental Soccer Association in Springfield engenders a riot, Homer buys a gun to 'protect' his family. When her requests that Homer dispose of the weapon fail, Marge takes herself and the kids away to the 'Sleep-Easy'motel.

Blackboard: Everyone is tired of that Richard Gere story.

Couch: The Simpsons butts are on fire: they sooth them in a water-filled couch.

What's been cut?: Well, the entire episode, actually. At the time of writing SKY hadn't shown it, but FOX had issued it on video on the *Too Hot for TV* compilation. It may be shown during 2000. Or not. What's extraordinary is that this is clearly an anti-firearms show which SKY have chosen to censor on the most dubious of grounds. Or so they can get you to pay for a video – your choice...

Bart Star (5F03) 09 November1997

Homer signs Bart up for peewee football, with Ned Flanders as coach. Homer constantly barracks Ned, and ends up coaching himself, whereupon his misplaced desire to encourage his son makes him replace a better quarterback with Bart, leading to the first defeat for the team. Eventually, after faking injury for the good of the team, Bart tells Homer that he quits. They make up, but when Chief Wiggum turns up with a warrant for team lynchpin Nelson Muntz they both have a hard decision to make.

Guest Stars: Roy Firestone, Mike Judge and Joe Namath.

Blackboard: I did not invent Irish dancing.

Couch: The Simpsons sit on the couch and are crushed into a small square block as the couch turns auto-crusher.

The Two Mrs. Nahasapeemapetilons (5F04) 16 November1997

As Apu finally gains popularity as a swinging bachelor his mother tells him it is time for his arranged marriage. Taking Homer's advice Apu claims to have already married Marge Simpson – but then his mother visits to meet her son's 'bride'.

Guest Stars: January Hooks and Andrea Martin.

Couch: The Simpsons are spray-painted onto the couch by Bart who adds an 'El Barto' signature, laughs and runs off.

Lisa the Skeptic (5F05) 23 November1997

When a skeleton with abnormal bone structures growing from the shoulders is uncovered during an archaeological survey, the people of Springfield conclude the remains are that of an angel. Except for one Lisa Simpson, who leads a rationalist attack on it that enrages the town. The 'angel' disappears from Homer's garage (where he's been running a pay-per-view operation) and appears on a nearby hillside with the words 'The End Will Come At Sundown' carved into it. What will come will challenge Lisa's scepticism.

Guest Stars: Stephen Jay Gould and Phil Hartman.

Blackboard: I will not tease Fatty.

Couch: The Simpsons rush in to find the couch is in a sauna occupied by three men in towels. They leave as one of the old men throws water on the hot rocks.

Realty Bites (5F06) 07 December 1997

Marge becomes the worst real estate agent in history when her honesty loses lucrative sales. She finally sells the least popular house in Springfield, the site of a grisly murder years previously. Meanwhile the hot-rod convertible that Homer buys at the local police auction is the former property of the marvellous (hey, it's my opinion) Snake who will do anything to get his property back.

Guest Stars: Phil Hartman.

Blackboard: There was no Roman god named "Farticus."

Couch: As the Simpsons sit, a live action human hand reaches into the screen and spins the picture around. When it stops the picture has been distorted like the pictures from a spin art booth.

Miracle on Evergreen Terrace (5F07) 21 December 1997

When Bart burns (or to be precise *melts*) the family's Christmas presents during an early morning raid on the Christmas tree, he's scared into claiming that they were stolen. Springfield flocks round to help, but unfortunately the truth comes out and the Simpsons become the most hated family in town.

Guest Stars: Alex Trebek.

Blackboard: Rudolph's red nose is not alcohol-related.

Couch: The Simpsons rush in and sit. The camera pulls back to reveal they are inside a snow globe held by giant hands. The globe is shaken and the camera zooms in to show the family looking around at the snow.

All Singing, All Dancing (5F24) 04 January 1998

The annual clip show is fired by Bart and Homer's disappointment at finding the Clint Eastwood film *Paint Your Wagon*, is actually a musical. Song and dance moments from seasons past ensue…

Guest Stars: George Harrison.

Couch: The Simpsons come in on a moving floor; they all make it to the couch except for Homer who falls and says 'Marge, stop this crazy thing!' George Jetson-style.

Bart Carny (5F08) 11 January 1998

Big-hearted Homer offers a carnival worker and his son a place to stay (well, he has cost them their jobs). Unfortunately the carnies like the house so much that they evict the Simpsons from their own property. Homer then tries to outsmart them…

Guest Stars: Jim Varney.

Couch: As the Simpsons go to sit, Nelson Muntz pulls the couch back, and they sit on the floor as Nelson delivers his trademark 'Ha ha.'

The Joy of Sect (5F23) 08 February 1998

When Homer is lured into the Movementarian cult (by free stuff) can the rest of Springfield be far behind? Marge realises that the cult's leader is only interested in money and along with Willie and Ned Flanders has to deprogram her family.

Blackboard: Shooting paintballs is not an art form.

Couch: Tiny versions of the Simpsons come in and try to scale the couch: Santa's Little Helper takes Homer away in his mouth, screaming.

Das Bus (5F11) 15 February 1998

When Bart, Lisa and their classmates become stranded on a deserted island and the dreams of tree houses and monkey butlers fail, they find they must fight for survival. Homer starts an internet business (without the hassle of actually going on the internet of course) and attracts unwanted attention from Bill Gates…

Guest Stars: James Earl Jones and Jack Ong.

Couch: Everyone is a frog (Maggie a tadpole) jumping to a lily pad; Homer turns on the TV with his tongue.

The Last Temptation of Krust (5F10) 22 February 1998

After blowing it big-style at a benefit concert with non-PC jokes Krusty realises that he has to move with the times and becomes an 'alternative' comedian. But there's a Canyonero in his future…

Guest Stars: Jay Leno, Steven Wright, Janeane Garofalo, Bobcat Goldthwait and Bruce Baum plus Hank Williams, Jr. (singing the

Canyonero theme song).

Blackboard: Pain is not the cleanser.

Couch: The Simpsons' butts are on fire: they sooth them in a water-filled couch.

Dumbbell Indemnity (5F12) 01 March 1998

Homer is enlisted in an insurance fraud when Moe goes broke wining and dining his new (only?) love Renee. The scam is so simple a child could pull it off: 'steal' Moe's car and park it across the train line while Moe and Renee are on the Police Charity Cruise. Homer stops for a drive in, misses the train, tries his own way of disposing of the car and ends up in jail…

Guest Stars: Helen Hunt.

Blackboard: Silly String is not a nasal spray.

Couch: The Simpsons sit on the couch and are crushed into a small square block as the couch turns auto-crusher.

Lisa the Simpson (4F24) 08 March 1998

When Lisa finds she can't figure out a brainteaser that even Nelson can solve, and a series of incidents seem to show she's losing her intelligence, the helpful Grandpa Simpson tells her that all Simpsons progressively lose their intelligence, and Lisa tries to adjust to life as a dolt. Jasper freezes himself in Apu's freezer as a substitute for cryogenics and Apu swiftly turns Kwik-E-Mart into a freakshow to capitalise on it.

Couch: A giant vine bursts into the middle of the room; the Simpsons sprout on it as fruit or vegetables.

This Little Wiggy (5F13) 22 March 1998

Marge feels sorry for the half-witted Ralph Wiggum and arranges a 'play-date' with Bart, to Bart's endless joy. When Bart learns that Chief Wiggum has a master key for every store in Springfield, and for the abandoned penitentiary, electric chair hi-jinks are not far behind…

Guest Stars: Phil Hartman.

Blackboard: I was not told to do this.

Couch: The Simpsons are spray-painted onto the couch by Bart who adds an 'El Barto' signature, laughs and runs off.

Simpson Tide (3G04) 29 March 1998

Needing a job after a near meltdown Homer joins the Naval reserve, where a series of blunders leaves him in charge of a submarine. He promptly guides it into soviet waters, and is branded a traitor by the media. Bart gets his ear pierced, which initially makes Homer angry but later saves his life…

Guest Stars: Rod Steiger and Michael Carrington.
Blackboard: My butt does not deserve a website.
Couch: A parody of *The Rocky and Bullwinkle Show* credit sequence.

The Trouble With Trillions (5F14) 05 April 1998

Homer completes his tax return with his usual attention to veracity. The document accidentally falls into the severe audit bin, he is arrested for fraud and forced to go undercover for the IRS. When he finds himself retrieving a trillion dollar bill stolen by Monty Burns, little does he think his destiny lies in Cuba.

Guest Stars: Paul Winfield.

Blackboard: I will not demand what I'm worth. (This is a reference to the cast asking for more money)

Couch: The Simpsons rush in to find the couch is in a sauna occupied by three men in towels. They leave as one of the old men throws water on the hot rocks.

Girly Edition (5F15) 19 April 1998

When Krusty has to surrender ten minutes of his show for an 'educational' kids news segment Lisa ends up as the anchorwoman for it. She is soon upstaged by the charismatic Bart, who ups the ante with the populist (and largely faked) 'Bart's People,' a human interest segment. Homer discovers that the disabled can get helper monkeys and uses his father to obtain Mojo. Soon it's Mojo that needs help.

Couch: As the Simpsons sit, a live action human hand reaches into the screen and spins the picture around. When it stops the picture has been distorted like the pictures from a spin art booth.

Trash of the Titans (5F09) 26 April 1998

Homer commits a serious faux pas by insulting the local garbage men, who terminate his trash pick-up. Homer runs against the current sanitation commissioner with the slogan 'Can't Somebody Else Do It?', promising round the clock garbage pickup amongst other things. As the paper says 'Simpson Wins In Landslide – Says Crazy Promises the Key'. Soon Homer has to pay for the promises.

Guest Stars: Steve Martin and U2.

Blackboard: I will not mess with the opening credits. (This appears in place of the couch opening; the rest of the family runs into the classroom)

Couch: Everyone except Bart runs into the living room to find it replaced with Bart's classroom, where he is writing 'I Will Not Mess With The Opening Credits' on the blackboard.

What's been cut?: The use of 'wankers' by Adam Clayton and Monty Burns. Wankers doesn't have the same meaning in the USA as in Britain.

King of the Hill (5F16) 03 May 1998

Homer embarrasses Bart by collapsing during a 'Capture The Flag' game at a church picnic and joins a gym, where a handy Rainier Wolfcastle helps him work out. When Wolfcastle turns down the makers of Powersauce sports bars offer to climb The Murderhorn to promote their product, a newly-fit Homer is standing in the wings, ready to attempt the certain-death feat.

Guest Stars: Brendan Fraser and Steven Weber.

Couch: The Simpsons rush in and sit. The camera pulls back to reveal they are inside a snow globe held by giant hands. The globe is shaken and the camera zooms in to show the family looking around at the snow.

Lost Our Lisa (5F17) 10 May 1998

Bart glues novelty items to his face using a glue he was given by Homer. Predictably enough it's permanent. As a result Marge (in rushing Bart to hospital mode) can't take Lisa to the last day of the Springsonian Museum's 'Treasures of Isis' exhibition. Desperate to go, Lisa cons Homer into letting her go by herself. She boards the wrong bus and, while the penny drops with Homer, becomes lost in the wrong part of town.

Blackboard: I am not the new Dalai Lama.

Couch: As the Simpsons go to sit, Nelson Muntz pulls the couch back, and they sit on the floor as Nelson delivers his trademark 'Ha ha.'

Natural Born Kissers (5F18) 17 May 1998

After an encounter with danger Homer and Marge find their sex life is ignited by dangerous situations. Subsequently they get plenty. Bart and Lisa find the alternate ending to Casablanca with a metal detector. It's *not* an improvement.

Blackboard: I was not the inspiration for "Kramer". (This episode was first shown just after the last episode of *Seinfeld*)

Couch: Everyone is a frog (Maggie a tadpole) jumping to a lily pad; Homer turns on the TV with his tongue.

Season Ten (1998-1999)

Lard of the Dance (5F20) 23 August 1998

Homer learns that waste kitchen grease can be sold and decides to make his grease fortune. Lisa is asked to introduce a new student Alex Whitney to the school. Alex is older than her years and soon has Lisa's friends dancing attendance on her, to Lisa's disgust. Meanwhile Homer has his eyes on the school's waste canteen grease, unaware that

Groundskeeper Willie regards it as his retirement fund, and is heading for a head on collision with the school dance.

Lard of the Dance was originally scheduled for season 10, but Fox broadcast it as a 'summer original' for promotional reasons.

Guest Stars: Lisa Kudrow.

Couch: As the Simpsons go to sit, Nelson Muntz pulls the couch back, and they sit on the floor as Nelson delivers his trademark 'Ha ha.'

The Wizard of Evergreen Terrace (5F21) 20 September 1998

Homer realises that he has lived for half of his life expectancy and hasn't accomplished anything. He looks to Thomas Edison for inspiration and decides to become an inventor.

Guest Stars: William Daniels.

Blackboard: I will not file frivolous lawsuits.

Couch: The Simpsons have to work their way past a number of Springfieldians, who are sitting in chairs in front of the couch, as if in a movie theatre. Homer takes a handful of Comic Book Guy's popcorn.

Bart, the Mother (5F22) 27 September 1998

While playing with Nelson Muntz's air gun Bart accidentally kills a mother bird, to his Mother's disgust. To try to win her approval he raises the mother's eggs on his own. Unfortunately when they hatch they turn out to be Bolivian Tree Lizards, a sort of lizard cuckoo, and if Bart doesn't give his charges up to be killed, the town's bird population may not survive.

Guest Stars: Phil Hartman.

Couch: Two firemen carry the couch and catch The Simpsons falling from above – except Homer, who falls through the floor leaving a Homer-shaped hole in it.

Treehouse of Horror IX (AABF01) 25 October 1998

The annual gorefest starts with a version of the standard credits from the point where Bart skateboards in over Homer's car: this time he hits his head on the garage door and collapses. Lisa runs into him with her bike, precipitating a pile up where everybody dies…

Hell Toupée

In a parody of films like *The Beast with Five Fingers,* where the transplanted hands of a killer force their new owner to kill, Homer has Snake's hair transplanted onto his head and must avenge its former owner.

The Terror of Tiny Toon

Using plutonium from Homer's toolbox to power the TV remote,

Bart and Lisa are transported into the Itchy & Scratchy Halloween special, with predictably bloody results. Poochie (from *The Itchy & Scratchy & Poochie* show) makes a second appearance in *The Simpsons.*

Starship Poopers

Maggie's father turns out to be the alien Kang, and he wants her back. They try to resolve the issue on the *Jerry Springer Show.* As who wouldn't?

Guest Stars: Regis Philbin, Kathie Lee Gifford, Jerry Springer, Ed McMahon and Robert Englund.

Blackboard: The Simpsons Halloween Special IX. (painted on the board in blood!)

Couch: Freddy Krueger of *A Nightmare on Elm Street* and Jason Voorhees of *Friday the 13th* sit on the couch wondering where the Simpsons are.

When You Dish Upon a Star (5F19) 08 November1998

When Homer becomes personal assistant to the husband and wife team of Alec Baldwin and Kim Basinger, who have come to Springfield to get away from it all, it's not long before he blabs all. Rejected by them he opens the Museum of Hollywood Jerks in a Winnebago.

Guest Stars: Ron Howard, Brian Grazer, Alec Baldwin & Kim Basinger.

Blackboard: butt.butt is not my e-mail address. (Originally this was the more comprehensible 'butt.com', but sadly there *is* a 'butt.com')

Couch: Marge carries in a laundry basket and produces flat versions of the other members of the family from it, hanging them on a clothesline.

D'oh-In in the Wind (AABF02) 15 November1998

Determining that his middle initial stands for 'Jay' from a mural at a commune his mother once lived at, Homer decides to become a hippie. He adopts two of his mother's old friends who now run a juice business and, basically, destroys their lives.

Guest Stars: George Carlin and Martin Mull.

Blackboard: No one cares what my definition of 'is' is.

Couch: The Simpsons sit on the couch and a safety bar comes down in front of them as the couch turns into an amusement park ride.

Lisa Gets an A (AABF03) 22 November1998

While Homer raises a baby lobster to save money, Lisa fails to study for an upcoming test, due to being at home with a cold playing Bart's video game. Lisa cheats and her grade qualifies the school for financial aid. When she tells the truth, Superintendent Chalmers asks her to forget about it so the school can have the cash. Lisa has to decide whether to do wrong or deprive the school of much needed money. Happily there are some cynical adults around to help her out.

Blackboard: I will not scream for ice cream.

Couch: The Simpsons sit on the couch and hair dryers come down over their heads. When they are raised they all have someone else's hair. The weight of Marge's hair causes Maggie to tip over.

Homer Simpson in: "Kidney Trouble" (AABF04) 06 December 1998

When Homer refuses to stop the car so Grandpa Simpson can go to the toilet, Abe's kidneys explode and Homer is the only available donor. Homer, frightened for his life, takes to his heels for foreign climes, ending up on the ship of lost souls.

Blackboard: I am not a licensed hairstylist.

Couch: Everyone is a frog (Maggie a tadpole) jumping to a lily pad; Homer turns on the TV with his tongue.

Mayored to the Mob (AABF05) 20 December 1998

When Springfield's SF convention degenerates into a riot Homer rescues Mark Hamill and Mayor Quimby. He becomes the Mayor's new bodyguard and all is well until Homer discovers Fat Tony's mob is selling rat's milk to the town's schools. He forces Quimby to put a stop to it and the Mayor's life is in danger.

Guest Stars: Mark Hamill, of course, and Joe Mantegna.

Blackboard: "The President did it" is not an excuse. (This episode was first shown the day after President Clinton was impeached)

Couch: The Simpsons sit on the couch and are crushed into a small square block as the couch turns auto-crusher.

Viva Ned Flanders (AABF06) 10 January 1999

When Homer (and Springfield) discover that Ned Flanders is sixty years old, but looks younger due to his clean lifestyle, the general response is one of disgust. Ned begins to feel he's missed out and asks Homer to introduce him to the good life, showing Ned's powers of observation for what they are. Homer's introduction to *La vida loca* ends up in Las Vegas and marriage to two casino waitresses.

Guest Stars: The Moody Blues.

Blackboard: My mom is not dating Jerry Seinfeld.

Couch: As the Simpsons sit, a live action human hand reaches into the screen and spins the picture around. When it stops the picture has been distorted like the pictures from a spin art booth.

Wild Barts Can't Be Broken (AABF07) 17 January 1999

Springfield Elementary is trashed by Homer and drunken pals in celebration of victory by the Springfield Isotopes. The finest detective minds the town has to offer are brought to bear on the problem; the kids are blamed and a sunset curfew is brought into effect. The kids start a pirate radio station that begins to broadcast the adults' secrets, and before long the generation gap is a chasm.

Guest Stars: Cyndi Lauper.

Blackboard: Sherri does not "got back". I'm dumb – I have no idea what this means...

Couch: The Simpsons rush in wearing cowboy hats and 'ride' the back of the couch. The couch metamorphoses into a bomb which falls through the floor as the family ride it á la Slim Pickens in *Dr. Strangelove*.

Sunday, Cruddy Sunday (AABF08) 31 January 1999

Homer and Wally Kogen organise a bus trip to the Super Bowl for Homer's pals, but when they get there the tickets turn out to be counterfeit, and Homer has to find a way into the stadium. Which he does, eating all Rupert Murdoch's food in the process.

Guest Stars: Fred Willard, Troy Aikman, Rosie Grier, John Madden, Dan Marino, Pat Summerall, Dolly Parton and Rupert Murdoch.

Blackboard: I will not do the Dirty Bird. (The 'dirty bird' is the celebration dance of the Atlanta Falcons)

Couch: The family sit on the couch, which is floating on water. An iceberg hits is and it sinks; Maggie resurfaces on a cushion with the remote and changes the channel.

Homer to the Max (AABF09) 07 February 1999

A new television show, *Police Cops*, features a hip character called 'Homer Simpson' and our Homer enjoys a brief period of respect. Unfortunately the character is recast as a bumbling fat fool and Homer changes his name to Max Power to escape ridicule. His new name inspires him and he falls in with Springfield's rich and hip set while buying a monogrammed shirt, only for it all to end in a confrontation with the real 'Police Cops'.

Guest Stars: Ed Begley, Jr.

Couch: Marge carries in a laundry basket and produces flat versions of the other members of the family from it, hanging them on a clothesline.

I'm With Cupid (AABF11) 14 February 1999

Apu makes the other husbands of Springfield look bad when he showers his wife with Valentine's Day gifts to make up for his long absences at the Kwik-E-Mart. The men of Springfield band together to foil Apu's increasingly large gestures.

Guest Stars: January Hooks and Elton John.

Blackboard: Hillbillies are people too.

Couch: The Simpsons sit on the couch and hair dryers come down over their heads. When they are raised they all have someone else's hair. The weight of Marge's hair causes Maggie to tip over.

Marge Simpson in: "Screaming Yellow Honkers" (AABF10) 21 February 1999

Homer buys a Canyonero SUV (see *The Last Temptation of Krust*) but gives it to Marge when he discovers he bought the 'female's' model. Marge becomes a fully-fledged off-roader (Gripped! Sorted!) but succumbs to road rage, an aspect of her personality that comes in very handy when Homer becomes the victim of an enraged rhino.

Guest Stars: Hank Williams, Jr. (singing the Canyonero theme song).

Blackboard: Grammar is not a waste of time.

Couch: The Simpsons sit on the couch and a safety bar comes down in front of them as the couch turns into an amusement park ride.

Make Room for Lisa (AABF12) 28 February 1999

When Homer defaces the Bill of Rights (now the property of Omnitouch, a mobile phone company) Lisa's bedroom becomes a relay station for the business and she is forced to share a room with Bart. The stress of this leads her and Homer to sensory deprivation tanks where Lisa hallucinates she's Homer, and Homer has an incredible journey. Meanwhile, Marge treats the mobile phone calls as her personal soap opera.

Blackboard: I do not have diplomatic immunity. (Repeated from 9F20 *Marge In Chains*)

Couch: Two firemen carry the couch and catch the Simpsons falling from above – except Homer, who falls through the floor leaving a Homer-shaped hole in it.

Maximum Homerdrive (AABF13) 28 March 1999

Homer challenges a truck driver called Red to a beef-eating contest, and Red wins, but dies in the attempt. Homer vows to deliver his cargo, and makes off with Bart and Red's rig across country to deliver Red's shipment on time. Marge has her own craving for adventure and takes Lisa shopping at 'Señor Ding-Dong's Doorbell Fiesta'.

Blackboard: It does not suck to be you.

Couch: An adult Bart and Lisa and a young Homer (with a Maggie doll and a full head of hair) and Marge go to the couch; Homer takes the remote from Lisa, but Lisa slaps his hand and he gives it back.

Simpsons Bible Stories (AABF14) 04 April 1999

Reverend Lovejoy takes revenge on whoever (Homer of course) put a chocolate Easter Bunny in the collection plate by reading the Bible from the beginning, boring the Simpsons into dreamland. Marge dreams she and Homer are Adam and Eve, Lisa that she supports 'Moses' Milhouse, Homer that he's King Solomon (with a predictable resolution to dividing a pie) and Bart that he is David facing Goliath. Goliath II, that is.

Blackboard: I cannot absolve sins.

Couch: The Simpsons rush in and slip on banana peels, luckily ending up on the couch anyway. Maggie rushes on, slips and ends up in Marge's arms.

Mom and Pop Art (AABF15) 11 April 1999

Homer's mis-assembly of a garden barbecue is mistaken for art by a professional art dealer, and soon he is the darling of Eurotrash art-groupies. When his later work is rejected, Lisa telling him about Christo 'wrapping' the Reichstag (yes, really – look it up!) inspires him to a genuinely revolutionary piece of work.

Guest Stars: Isabella Rossellini and Jasper Johns.

Blackboard: A trained ape could not teach gym.

Couch: The Simpsons rush in wearing cowboy hats and 'ride' the back of the couch. The couch metamorphoses into a bomb which falls through the floor as the family ride it á la Slim Pickens in *Dr. Strangelove.*

The Old Man and the "C" Student (AABF16) 25 April 1999

Bart's obnoxious comedy routine costs Springfield the Olympic Games (it could happen!) and as a punishment he and his fellow students are given 20 hours community service each. Bart takes the inmates of Grandpa's retirement home out for a day á la *One Flew Over The Cuckoo's Nest.* Meanwhile Homer has to get rid of the springs he bought to make Springfield's Olympic Mascot.

Guest Stars: Jack LaLanne.

Blackboard: Loose teeth don't need my help.

Couch: The Simpsons have to work their way past a number of Springfieldians, who are sitting in chairs in front of the couch, as if in a movie theatre. Homer takes a handful of Comic Book Guy's popcorn.

Monty Can't Buy Me Love (AABF17) 02 May 1999

Finding he has a public approval rating in the minus region Monty Burns gets Homer to work on his image (proving once again his amnesia where Homer is concerned). Failing, he decides to win the public's admiration by doing something really extraordinary – retrieving the legendary Loch Ness Monster.

Guest Stars: Michael McKean.

Blackboard: I have neither been there nor done that.

Couch: The Simpsons form a chorus line, and are joined by the Rockettes, circus animals, jugglers, trapeze artists, magicians, fire breathers and Santa's Little Helper (amongst others) for a musical spectacular.

What's been cut?: SKY cut a lot of simulated camera flashes, possibly in response to the panic over the *Pokémon* cartoon that caused epileptic fits in Japanese children.

They Saved Lisa's Brain (AABF18) 09 May 1999

Lisa writes a letter of disgust complaining about the riot engendered by a 'How Low Will You Go' contest and is invited to join the local MENSA society. When Mayor Quimby disappears under the (mistaken) assumption that all his corruption has come to light, the members find that under local law they can take over. Chaos and Stephen Hawking ensue.

Guest Stars: Stephen Hawking.

Blackboard: No one wants to hear from my armpits. (From 3F01 *Home Sweet Home-Diddily-Dum-Doodily*)

Couch: The family sit on the couch, which is floating on water. An iceberg hits is and it sinks; Maggie resurfaces on a cushion with the remote and changes the channel.

Thirty Minutes Over Tokyo (AABF20) 16 May 1999

After attending a mega-savings seminar the Simpsons go to Japan, buying up last minute cancellations. After losing their money they participate in a Japanese TV game show that specialises in humiliating studio contestants, in exchange for air fare back home.

Guest Stars: George Takei and Gedde Watanabe.

Blackboard: I am so very tired.

Couch: The Simpsons sit on the couch, which sucks them in like a paper shredder and passes them back out in strips.

Season Eleven (1999-2000)

The latest season is well up to the high standard set by previous seasons, and seems (with episodes like Bart's Little Helper*) to be going back to some of the earlier seasons for inspiration. There really doesn't seem to be any reason The Simpsons shouldn't go on forever – a personal terror for me having stuffed this much information into 96 pages. What if they ask me to update it in ten years time? I haven't seen the last few episodes of season eleven yet, so out of the kindness of my heart I've left spaces for you to put the Couch and Blackboard gags in. If you have a* really tiny pen, *that is…*

Beyond Blunderdome (AABF23) 26 September 1999

After Homer is the only person to agree with Mel Gibson that a remake of *Mr. Smith Goes to Washington* previewing in Springfield lacks sufficient violence, he becomes a Hollywood consultant. His first job? To help Gibson make an appropriately violent version of the classic film.

Guest Stars: Mel Gibson, Jack Burns and Karl Wiedergott.

Blackboard: Fridays are not "pants optional".

Couch: The Simpsons stop as the couch is occupied – by the Simpsons from *The Tracey Ullman Show*; all ten of the Simpsons run off screaming.

Brother's Little Helper (AABF22) 03 October 1999

Skinner threatens Bart with expulsion unless he goes on 'Focusyn,' a new drug touted to boost academic attention spans. It improves his behaviour in school for a time. That is until the side effects kick in. Then Springfield must face a tank-driving Bart Simpson...

Guest Stars: Mark McGwire.

Blackboard: Pork is not a verb.

Couch: The Simpsons are white and are covered with numbers 'paint by numbers' style; artists enter and paint in the colours.

Guess Who's Coming to Criticize Dinner? (AABF21) 24 October 1999

The Springfield Shopper's new restaurant critic? Homer J. With a little help from Lisa, Homer has a successful column on his hands, but his inflated ego leads him to write (well, instruct Lisa to write) more and more bad reviews. Soon the local restaurant owners decide it's Homer or them and hire a ruthless assassin – a French chef. This continues the grand Simpsons tradition of mocking the Brits for their teeth and the French for everything else that's bad in the world. *"A rude Frenchman, well I never!"* – Ned Flanders.

Guest Stars: Ed Asner.

Blackboard: I am not the last Don.

Couch: Marge erases the Matt Groening signature on the floor; Matt appears and rewrites it.

Treehouse of Horror X (BABF01) 31 October 1999

Those loveable aliens Kang and Kodos host the tenth annual scare the hell out of your kids episode. The end of *Life's a Glitch...* will probably induce nightmares in the very young, as Homer and Bart die in a kind of gruesome manner.

I Know What You Diddily-Iddily Did

When Marge accidentally runs Flanders over he apparently returns from the grave seeking revenge. Is that a wolfish grin he has?

Desperately Xeeking Xena

Bart and Lisa's get super powers when the police X-ray machine explodes and have to rescue Lucy Lawless from a mad collector (guess who?) who wants to add Xena to his haul of celebrities.

Life's A Glitch, Then You Die

When a Y2K meltdown destroys earth because Homer didn't debug the Springfield Nuclear Power Plant the survivors head for the stars. Except those on the wrong rocket.

Guest Stars: Dick Clark, Tom Arnold, Lucy Lawless and Frank Welker.

Couch: The Simpsons all appear as characters from previous Halloween Specials; Maggie disintegrates Lisa.

E-I-E-I-(ANNOYED GRUNT) (AABF19) 07 November 1999

Homer moves the family to Grandpa's old farm (which burnt down in *Grandpa vs. Sexual Inadequacy,* surely?) and he and Bart devise 'Tomacco', an addictive cross between Tobacco and Tomatoes. If you missed it '(annoyed grunt)' is the way the scripts refer to Homer's unique 'doh' sound.

Blackboard: I did not win the Nobel Fart prize.

Couch: The couch and environs is roped off like a club. The family runs up and a bouncer allows Marge, Maggie, Bart, and Lisa in but refuses Homer.

Hello Gutter, Hello Fadder (BABF02) 14 November 1999

When Homer's bowls a perfect game his ten-pin wizardry lands him instant celebrity status. His newfound fame results in appearances on *The Springfield Squares* and a *Penn & Teller Special*. Unfortunately he finds that 'instant' is also a measurement of time.

Guest Stars: Penn Jillette, Teller, Ron Howard, Nancy O'Dell and Pat O'Brien.

Blackboard: I won't use no double negatives.

Couch: A cement truck deposits a load of cement at the bottom of the couch. It forms into the Simpsons. Homer's head cracks and drops off.

Eight Misbehavin' (BABF03) 21 November 1999

Apu learns that he's about to become a dad eight times over. However, he and Manjula find that caring for octuplets is a trying task until a zoo owner offers a lending hand, signing the octuplets to a contract for several shows a day...

Guest Stars: January Hooks and Butch Patrick.

Blackboard: Indian burns are not our cultural heritage.

Couch: The Simpsons run in and sit on the couch, as usual. Suddenly the couch and the wall behind it revolves, hiding the Simpsons and revealing Ned Flanders, chained upside-down to the other side of the wall. Vincent Price stands next to him, laughing evilly.

Take My Wife, Sleaze (BABF05) 28 November1999

When Homer wins a Harley-Davidson motorcycle at the Greaser's Café, a 50's-themed restaurant what more natural than he should form a biker gang, the Hell's Satans? Unfortunately the real Hell's Satans, led by Meathook and Ramrod, take exception to this, trashing the Simpsons' house and taking Marge with them. Homer has to get Marge back – it's the Biker code.

Guest Stars: John Goodman, Henry Winkler and NRBQ.

Blackboard: I can't see dead people. (a reference to the movie *Sixth Sense*)

Couch: The Simpsons sit on the couch which sucks them in like a paper shredder and passes them back out in strips.

Grift of the Magi (BABF07) 19 December 1999

A sinister toy company unveils the next 'Tickle Me Elmo'-style fad to Springfield's Christmas shoppers.

Fat Tony's involvement in Springfield Elementary leads to it going broke. The children rejoice until Jim Hope and Kid First Industry (KFI) buys the school and privatises it. Strangely, all the lessons now seem to revolve around toys and marketing. Lisa and Bart investigate.

Guest Stars: Gary Coleman.

Blackboard: I will not sell my kidney on eBay.

Couch: Everybody slides down a fire pole – except Homer, who gets stuck in the hole in the ceiling.

Little Big Mom (BABF04) 9 January 2000

Lisa has to stand in for Marge, who's broken her leg in a skiing accident. Lisa tries reasoning but Homer and Bart ignore her and Evergreen Terrace again becomes a pig sty. Lisa decides to play a trick on the lazy menfolk and persuades them that they have leprosy. This works so well that Ned Flanders arranges for Homer and Bart to be sent to a leper colony in Hawaii. Meanwhile, Marge discovers the wonders of shiatsu massage in the hospital.

Guest Stars: Elwood Edwards.

Blackboard: I will not create art from dung.

Couch: Everybody is a crash test dummy; the couch crashes into the TV.

Faith Off (BABF06) 16 January 2000

Bart is impressed by a faith healer called Brother Faith, who empowers him to remove a superglued bucket from Homer's head (don't ask). Bart decides to become a healer and heals several Springfield residents before causing Milhouse to be hit by a car. Bart swears off faith healing for good, but when the field goal kicker for Springfield University injures his ankle during an important game, healing (and pain killers) beckon.

Guest Stars: Joe Mantegna and Don Cheadle.

Blackboard: I will stop phoning it in.

Couch: A psychiatrist is sitting next to the couch; Homer lies on it and says "Oh, Doctor, I'm crazy."

The Mansion Family (BABF08) 23 January 2000

Springfield's oldest citizen, Montgomery Burns decides to take a trip with Mr. Smithers to the Mayo Clinic for a complete check-up and asks the Simpson family to look after his mansion (that memory loss again). When Homer decides to throw a party aboard Burns' yacht, *Gone Fission,* disaster beckons and Homer and crew are taken hostage by a group of pirates... Will they survive? Is Burn's house in one piece? The Shadow knows...

Guest Stars: Britney Spears.

Blackboard: Class clown is not a paid position.

Couch: An adult Bart and Lisa and a young Homer (with a Maggie doll and a full head of hair) and Marge go to the couch; Homer takes the remote from Lisa, but Lisa slaps his hand and he gives it back.

Saddlesore Galactica (BABF09) 06 February 2000

Homer and Bart save a diving horse named Duncan during a trip to the State Fair. Bart decides to turn Duncan into a racehorse but he's too sensitive. Homer and Bart 'toughen him up' and he returns as a bad-boy rebel renamed Furious D, who intimidates all his competitors with his dyed hair and nose ring. Unfortunately the other jockeys are not what they seem...

Guest Stars: Bachman-Turner Overdrive (Randy Bachman, Trevor Denman and C.F. Turner as themselves) and Jim Cummings.

Blackboard: Substitute teachers are not scabs.

Couch: The Simpsons come on in karate gear and chop up the couch.

Alone Again, Natura-Diddly (BABF10) 13 February 2000

On the opening day of a new auto-racing track all of Springfield gathers to see the racing, but during the intermission, Maude Flanders is killed in an accident, and Ned needs to rebuild his life. Oh, look here comes Rachel Jordan, the lead singer of a Christian rock band...

Guest Stars: Shawn Colvin and Frank Welker.

Blackboard: My suspension was not "mutual".

Couch: The Simpsons are driving bumper cars; Homer is bumped by the others against the back wall.

Missionary: Impossible (BABF11) 20 February 2000

Fleeing from an angry PBS posse that includes Betty White, Mr. Rogers, the Teletubbies, and Oscar the Grouch (again, don't ask) Homer is got out of the country by the Reverend Lovejoy, on a Christian Relief plane bound for the South Pacific, where he acts as a missionary with predictable results. Back in Springfield Bart has taken over Homer's job at the Springfield Nuclear Power Plant.

Guest Stars: Betty White.

Blackboard: A belch is not an oral report.

Couch: The couch is in Evergreen Terrace subway station; everybody gets aboard a train.

Pygmoelian (BABF12) 27 February 2000

When Moe's face is deemed so ugly that his photo in a calendar is covered with a giant sticker, he invests in some much-needed plastic surgery, emerging with smooth good looks. Moe resumes his acting career (remember?) on *It Never Ends*, a soap opera he once tried out for. But when he discovers that his character is about to be written out, sabotage beckons...

Blackboard: Dodgeball stops at the gym door.

Couch: Marge erases the Matt Groening signature on the floor; Matt appears and rewrites it.

Bart to the Future (BABF13) 19 March 2000

Like Lisa (in *Lisa's Wedding)* Bart is afforded a glimpse of his future, courtesy the wise Native American casino magnate this time. Thirty years in the future Bart is sleeping on Ralph Wiggum's couch, trying his hardest to make it as a rock guitarist. His sister is President of the United States and Bart decides to move into the White House, which will start off as a negative, and end as a positive, for Madame President.

Blackboard: "Non-Flammable" is not a challenge.

Couch: The couch and environs is roped off like a club. The family runs up and a bouncer allows Marge, Maggie, Bart, and Lisa in but refuses Homer.

Days of Wine and D'oh'ses (BABF14) 9 April 2000

Barney goes on the wagon after seeing a videotape of himself drunk while Bart and Lisa learn the ups and downs of photography in a contest held by the local telephone company.

Blackboard: I was not touched "there" by an angel.

Couch: The Simpsons stop as the couch is occupied – by the Simpsons from *The Tracey Ullman Show*; all ten Simpsons run off screaming.

Kill the Alligator and Run (BABF16) 30 April 2000

Homer and the family spend their spring break vacation avoiding the Florida authorities after running over Florida's beloved alligator Captain Jack.

Guest Stars: Kid Rock, Joe C., Charlie Rose and Robert Evans.

Blackboard:

Couch:

Last Tap Dance in Springfield (BABF15) 7 May 2000

Lisa is enrolled in a dance studio run by former a child actress Vicki Valentine. What will happen when Lisa outshines her teacher?

Blackboard:

Couch:

It's a Mad, Mad, Mad, Mad, Marge (BABF18) 14 May 2000

A young woman staying with the Simpsons starts to one-up Marge in the mothering stakes.

Blackboard:

Couch:

Behind the Laughter (BABF19) 21 May 2000

What if the Simpsons were a real family who portrayed themselves on TV? Explore the off-stage lives of the Simpson family – money, drugs, celebrity and supermodels.

Guest starring *Willie Nelson.*

Blackboard:

Couch:

Resources (well, largely stuff you can buy, really)

Videos

The following videos were issued in the UK, and the fine gentlemen at www.blackstar.co.uk have many of them at very reasonable prices (and I'm not just saying that – the week I checked they had 20% off and free delivery).

Bart The General
Bart Wars
Call of the Simpsons
Crime And Punishment
Crime And Punishment / Sex, Lies And The Simpsons (Double Pack)
Dancin' Homer / Old Money
Dead Putting Society / Oh Brother
Homer's Night Out
Krusty Gets Busted
Life In The Fast Lane (aka Born To Be Wild)
Moaning Lisa
Mr Lisa Goes To Washington / Separate Vocations
Sex, Lies And The Simpsons
Simpsons Against The World
Simpsons, The – The Dark Secrets Of Springfield Murder Mysteries
The Last Temptation Of Homer (previously Homer Alone)
The Simpsons
The Simpsons – Greatest Hits
The Simpsons' Christmas Special / Bart Gets An 'F'
The Simpsons Go To Hollywood
The Simpsons, – Season 1 Box Set
Three Men And A Comic Book / Blood Feud
Too Hot For TV
Treehouse Of Horror / Simpson And Delilah
Two Cars In Every Garage / Brush With Greatness
Viva Los Simpsons
War Of The Simpsons / Lisa's Substitute

Comics and Books

The Bongo line of comics is reprinted in the UK by Titan: Subscriptions and Back Issues enquiries on 01536 763631. In the US check your local comic shop.

You can also get the US issues on import from: Forbidden Planet (mail order) at 71 New Oxford Street, London, WC1A 1DG. tel: +44 0207 497 2150 and Planet Warehouse at PO Box 369, Maldon, Essex CM9 4XD tel: +44 01621 877244 (Planet are recommended for comics fans – they often have large amounts of unfeasibly cheap merchandise for sale).

In addition the following graphic novels are collections of the Bongo material, and are published by HarperCollins in the US and Titan in the UK:

Simpsons Comics: A-go-go
Simpsons Comics: Big Bonanza
Simpsons Comics: Extravaganza
Simpsons Comics: Featuring Bartman
Simpsons Comics: On Parade
Simpsons Comics: Simps-o-rama
Simpsons Comics: Spectacular
Simpsons Comics: Strike Back
Simpsons Comics: Wingding

The following are books of various kinds related to the show:

The Simpsons : A Complete Guide to Our Favourite Family by Matt Groening
The Simpsons Forever by Matt Groening
The Simpsons' Guide to Springfield by Matt Groening(Illustrator)

These three books (published by HarperCollins in Europe and HarperPerennial in the US) are collectively the equivalent of the book you hold in your hand. In their favour is they are bigger, in colour, more detailed and look beautiful. Against them: they only go up to season ten and they're relatively expensive. *The Complete Guide* covers seasons 1 – 8, *Forever* seasons 9 & 10 and *The Guide to Springfield* is, well, a guide to the fair city of Springfield. Well worth buying if you're really into the show.

Bart Simpson's Guide to Life by Matt Groening, HarperCollins
The Simpsons' Fun in the Sun Book by Matt Groening, HarperCollins

The Simpsons Rainy Day Fun Book by Matt Groening, HarperCollins
Cartooning with the Simpsons by Matt Groening, HarperCollins
Simpson's Uncensored Family Album by Matt Groening HarperCollins
Homer Simpson's Guide to Being a Man by Matt Groening, HarperCollins

These all come under the heading of 'comedy tie ins' and are all described by their titles. Apart from *Homer Simpson's Guide to Being a Man* (which I haven't yet seen) they are all good, probably due to Groening's personal involvement.

Simpsons (Behind the Creation of Series) by Bob Italia, Abdo Pub Co

An awful book that you should avoid at all costs, especially as the damn thing costs a fortune.

I Can't Believe It's a Bigger and Better Updated Unofficial Simpsons Guide by Warren Martyn, Adrian Wood, Virgin Publishing

An unofficial guide, much like this one at twice the price for twice the pages. You pays your money...

Bart Simpson's Treehouse of Horrors by Matt Groening, HarperCollins

Collection of Bongo/Titan comics grouped around the Halloween theme issues. Very good.

Unauthorized Guide to The Simpsons Collectibles by Robert W. Getz, Schiffer Publishing
Collecting Simpsons! An Unofficial Guide to Merchandise from The Simpsons by William D. Larue, KML Enterprises Publishing.

If you're into collecting Simpsons' stuff of all colours and hues these books are for you.

Web Resources

Apart from a number of websites and newsgroups that distribute illegal binaries of the shows the show and the internet seem to have a love-love relationship going on, although as with *Buffy The Vampire Slayer* Fox have had many sites shut down. There are far too many Simpsons sites to list here, but here are the edited highlights.

http://www.snpp.com/ – The Simpsons Archive

You may never get further than this site, certainly the best Simpsons site and possibly the best site related to TV in the world. You think I'm joking – I'm not. Everything from episode summaries to FAQs, lists, News, Links and other handy stuff. It's hosted on-line by Gary Goldberg of DigiMark, who the world owes a big vote of thanks (as does the current author). It's been on line since 1994 and receives 5.5 million hits *monthly!* No wonder the official site comes second...

http://thesimpsons.com/ – the official Fox site for the show

Here you can get your own free internet access and email @thesimpsons.com. With games, an online store for merchandise, episode guides and lots more, including information about upcoming episodes. Be warned that the international shipping charge for the store is a whopping $19.95 for orders under $100 and $49.95 for orders above $100. On the other hand there is some nice stuff in the store... The site itself is well designed, easy to navigate and attractive.

http://members.aol.com/bartfan/ – Collecting The Simpsons

A marvellous site for those who collect all things Simpson. You'll find value guides for Action Figures, Audio & Video, Balloons, Simpsons Saving Banks, Simpsons Books, Simpsons Cards, Clothing, Comic Books, Simpsons Dolls, Simpsons Games, Holiday Items, Household, Key Rings, Pin, Stick & Hang, School, Writing , Watches and loads of news, photos and an archive of back issues.

http://www.synergizedsolutions.com/simpsons/ – Pick's Tribute to *The Simpsons*

Articles on the people behind the show – Matt Groening, the voice artists, how an episode is made – and guides to how to find merchandise on the net etc. Very nice site.

http://springfield.simplenet.com/folder/ - *The Simpsons* Folder

This site has lots information, collections of articles, photographs, animation art, cels and over 600 scanned Simpsons images from books, magazines and much more. Well worth a look.

http://www.milpool.com/ - Evergreen Terrace

Trivia, chatrooms, fan fiction (Simpsons episodes you've only imagined...), history and articles about the show.

http://www.labyrinth.net.au/~kwyjibo/ - The Simpsonian Institute

The site owner Tammy Hocking says this is "for serious fans, with behind-the-scenes info (almost impossible to find), an episode guide, links to other Simpsons sources, articles on the show, and pictures of the cast and crew." And who am I to disagree?

http://www.deprofundis.freeserve.co.uk/main11.html

This is 'The Snipsons' site aimed at all viewers of *The Simpsons* in the United Kingdom and Europe – the purpose being to provide a comprehensive listing of scenes and quotes that featured in the original episodes, as shown in the USA, but have been cut or edited permenantly or temporarily by SKY and the BBC when aired in the UK. The site is a first rate resource where you can find out much more about the censoring of *The Simpsons* than I can in a book this size – give it a visit. Go on...

You should also check out alt.tv.simpsons, the main newsgroup for the show. Sometimes a bit argumentative, but very good for keeping up with the show and how it's seen in the USA.
